Why I Didn't Leave

When Abusive Relationships Hold Us Hostage

Why I Didn't Leave

When Abusive Relationships Hold Us Hostage

Courtney Miller

Table of Contents

Chapter Nine

Preface

In these chapters, we will uncover lies that have held many captive in toxic, unhealthy, and abusive relationships. A vast majority of the accounts are from my personal experience, but I have incorporated other stories as well. Some are intimate partner stories, while others are from parent/child relationships. Some are from employer/employee interactions. Some are stories I have heard first-hand, and others I have witnessed in person. Several of them are real-life nightmares my friends and family members have lived through. As you read these accounts, please remember they aren't just stories. They are someone's life.

These life experiences are graphic and depictive. I have done my best to warn you when the deep, heavy, and comfortable events are about to happen. No matter where you find yourself picking up this book and reading these pages, please know these chapters can be triggering. They can cause outbursts of emotions you didn't realize still reside inside you.

Please take your time as you read. This isn't a book to rush or skim. If you're reading it for yourself or with someone else in mind, please know there is help out there!

To the men: According to The National Coalition Against Domestic Violence, 1 in 4 women and 1 in 9 men have experienced domestic violence from an intimate partner. Abusive and unhealthy relationships are no respecter of persons. Toxicity doesn't care about your age, gender, or ethnicity. I believe men are more susceptible to endure abusive environments (in dating, marriage, careers, etc.) in silence because they do not always have someone in their corner who believes they could be abused. People think because they are "men" they couldn't be a victim of an unhealthy relationship. This notion could not be further from the truth.

So, to the men, I believe you, and I see you. As a female author, I have tried my best to keep a neutral perspective about gender, but if you read anything to the contrary, please forgive any feminine nuances. These chapters, these truths, and this healing are just as much yours as they are your female counterparts'.

Resources: If you or anyone you know is in a domestic violent relationship, please call the National Domestic Violence Hotline at 1-800-799-7233. If you or anyone you know has experienced sexual assault, please contact the National Sexual Assault Hotline at 800.656.HOPE.

Pause, Ponder, Prayer: After each chapter, there will be a reflection section. The *pause* sections invite you to gather your thoughts and identify your emotions from the previously read chapter. I recommend writing your thoughts and answering the questions in a journal. Our home church has a saying that "Paper never forgets" (One Church of Caddo Mills), and when you look back on our time together, you can track your progress and healing chapter by chapter.

The *ponder* sections ask thought-provoking questions in order to navigate and understand what you just read.

The *prayer* sections are words I specifically prayed over you as the reader. I encourage you to make the prayers personalized. When I say, "my friend," insert your name. When I refer to overarching issues, I implore you to write out your specific requests. Lastly, I pray the accompanying Scriptures anchor you to healing and propel you onto the next chapter.

My Cheerleaders and Truth Tellers

Grant,

As I'm writing this you've chased Brin around outside for as long as possible. She can no longer be distracted by the outdoors. So now, you're listening to the noisy jungle animal book for the 100th time with her. Thank you, thank you, thank you.

Thank you for being a raving Courtney Miller fan. Thank you for pausing your dreams and aspirations so I could pursue mine. Thank you for holding huge God-sized dreams for me and championing me to see bigger and better. You are the best husband, partner, friend, and parent, and I am honored to live this life with you.

I love you with all that I am. In everything, 100/100.

Brendar, Mallory, Emily, Abi, Kahla, Macie, Kayla, Raegan, Hailey, Dominique, and Michele,

Thank you all for believing in me. Thank you for encouraging me. Thank you for kicking me in the butt when I didn't want to write anymore—when I wanted to give up. Thank you for reminding me what the Lord says about me and His call on my life. Thank you for reminding me of the power, the breakthrough, and the healing in these chapters. Thank you for reminding me that the younger me needed to read this book, and now many others have the chance to find freedom in these pages. Thank you for all the caffeine you brought me. Thank you for the countless hours you have poured into Brinley so I could write.

My book launch team,

Thank you for reading and rereading these pages, and giving me honest and sometimes brutal feedback, edits, and revisions. Thank you for bathing this process in prayer. Thank you for your commitment even with your already busy lives. Your input was timely and valuable.

Thank you for always being my cheerleaders. My raving fans. My truth-tellers. My incredible friends and family. I love you BIG.

Introduction

How Did I End Up Here?

I sit here agonizing over the question that begs an answer. This is the question I was asked a million times over during the relationship. Even as I sit on the other side of it, I'm still asking and reeling over the same question. My head is spinning because I don't know.

I sit here writing, "How did this happen?" or better yet, "How did this happen again?"

Courtney, why didn't you leave?

Why didn't you leave when you were belittled, shamed, yelled at, and called names? Why didn't you leave when isolated, threatened, and silenced? Why did you ignore the tension when your opinion was hushed, when you had to defend everything, and when you felt pacifying was the only answer?

Did you think *if I just appease, the situation will get better? If I give in, this will all go away. If I ignore the warning signs, it won't actually come to pass.* Or did you believe they just needed your help? After all, you were trying to be there for them when no one else was. No one else would understand. They may be lost right now, but they are finding their way. You just have to hold on a little bit longer.

These thoughts consumed me until I began to unravel the lies holding me prisoner. Prisoner to my past. The lies that bound me to that person. That relationship. That job. That boss. That team. That coach. That family member.

Each of us has *that* person. The mention of their name conjures up a whirlwind of emotions. Stops you in your tracks. Even someone who simply looks like them leaves you frozen right there in the grocery store. Attached to that person, those memories, and the past are lies we continue to believe.

Friend, why did you stay?

Maybe you couldn't leave. Maybe you felt trapped. Stuck. Powerless.

I wish the answer was easy. I wish it wasn't complicated. I wish I could tell you why I stayed. Why I constantly walked on eggshells. Why I let them use, abuse, and exhaust me. I wish it all made sense. Why I allowed someone take my peace, my joy, and my security. Why I was robbed of my value and identity.

Unhealthy toxic relationships suck us in and leave us depleted. The lies we believe about ourselves and the situation we find ourselves in can be paralyzing, soul-crushing, and even traumatic. They leave us vulnerable and ashamed. These lies may even create strongholds in our lives. We buy into the delusion that we must protect that person and defend them when, in reality, we are the ones needing protection and defense. These toxic relationships create an imbalance of power, and the strongholds are called "strong" for a reason. They leave us feeling responsible for a burden that isn't ours to carry.

Unhealthy toxic relationships leave us wondering:

Who am I?

What is my opinion?

Do I even matter?

Why did this happen?

Will I ever find myself again?

I didn't leave because I didn't see it. I didn't realize it was a hostage situation. I didn't understand what was happening before it was too late, and I was too sucked in to leave unscathed. The lies of my unhealthy relationship were pervasive. They invaded every part of my life. The lies were suffocating, and they felt permanent. Time may have passed, and the relationship was over, but the ramifications were still raw and painful. I was still paying a price and still believing the lies.

It is my fault. I'm too dramatic. I overreacted. I'm not enough. If I just try harder. I'm too invested. I can't leave. I'm not smart. My ideas are worthless. This is as good as life gets. No one will understand. No one will love me again. I'm disposable. I'm replaceable. I'm unwanted and all alone.

I deserve this.

These are just some of the all-consuming lies that lurk from the past, deteriorate our present, and threaten our future. They were the lies that held me hostage in the relationship and the lies I didn't address once I left. Lies that needed to be challenged and crushed! We need reframing and rewiring not only to see but also to *believe* and *embody* the truth.

I invite you to journey with me to unpack the lies that kept me stuck in the worst relationship of my life. On the way, I hope you will learn how to avoid the toxic pitfalls I continuously found myself in, as well as learn how to heal mental wounds and emotional scarring. I will tell you how I calmed triggers and rediscovered my value and identity in Christ. Walk with me while we unravel the lies and put back the pieces to health; to reclaim what the Lord said about us in our past and STILL says about us now.

I do not claim to be an expert in relationships, nor do I pretend to have it all together. I'm not a licensed counselor or therapist. In fact, my degrees are in marketing and organizational leadership. But I did suffer in a controlling, narcissistic, and abusive relationship for several years. For a stint of time, I was the girl in that toxic relationship that everyone pitied. The girl they said deserved better and who they'd try to convince to leave. I have lived this life, and I know many of you have as well. Some of you are still living this life.

In writing this book, I am to let you know you are not alone and to offer my real-life experiences as examples to learn from. In addition, I have included statistics, studies, and websites further proving what I say to be true.

I'm passionate about encouraging others that healing awaits them even though they feel broken today. I get a rush of fulfillment when I see someone on the other side of their brokenness. When I see them transformed, mended and whole, and now empowering others to do the same, it makes all my pain and struggles worth it.

Margaret Feinberg says, "Practicing defiant joy is the declaration that the darkness does not and will not win." For me, practicing that defiant joy is not always being so serious. Yes, my past is rocky. There is a lot to cry about. And I did cry about it, but there is also much to laugh about. There is a lot to be joyful about. Throughout these stories, you'll see a glimpse of my joy, my humor, and my sassy attitude (God is still working on me).

However, my joy, humor, laughter, and even my sassy attitude do not negate or downplay the bad things that happened to me. They remind me who I am and more importantly whose I am. They remind me that death did not win. The darkness did not win. They remind me that through Christ, I am made in His image. They remind me that I am victorious!

I'm going to lead you through some of my darkest times. It's going to be raw. It's going to be messy. It may even be painful. But it's also going to be full of redemption. Full of grace. Full of forgiveness. And definitely full of hope. I pray that through these chapters, you process and heal from whatever unhealthy toxic relationships you've endured. I pray you'll discover the same redemption, grace, forgiveness, and hope that I did. And to empower you to embrace the healthy relationships that surround you now.

This is a book to unpack the clutter and chaos that leaves us befuddled from our previous relationships. This book exposes the lies we've believed about ourselves and what they said about us and to us. Those lies weigh us down and keep us bound.

This book provides a safe place for you to process the exhaustion, betrayal, and isolation you've felt for so long. It's an invitation to heal the parts of your soul that have been sucked dry. It's an opportunity to reclaim your identity, reestablish your values, and propel you to engage in healthy relationships moving forward.

Each of us has a story, and now it is time to tell mine.

Chapter One

It Wasn't Always Like This

We sat on my brown sectional one calm spring afternoon. I was on one side while my best friend sat on the other. She sat patiently, waiting for me to speak. We were alone for now, and I needed to start speaking. I didn't know how much time I had before he would return.

But I didn't know where to begin. I didn't know what to do. I didn't know where to go.

I wasn't looking for pity or sympathy. I was desperate and ready for change, but I didn't know where to start. I peered out the window, disheartened.

How could the sun shine vibrantly and the flowers bloom when my heart felt dull and my body withered?

"It's okay. Tell her."

The Holy Spirit had spoken to me a lot more lately. It's crazy how that happens when we actively seek Him. But I was afraid to say it out loud. I didn't want to say it and go back on my word again. I didn't want to declare it and then double back on my promise. I didn't want to let people down again.

I felt so weak. I would say I was done and ready to leave. My friends and family would cheer me on. They were always so proud of me when I packed my things up and left. But when I did leave, it was only temporary. I lost count of how many times I had said I would leave and never really left FOR GOOD. Even when the police had to get involved, I still went back.

Time would pass. I would leave an extra set of clothes at his place. Then I'd leave my toothbrush. Then he'd clear out a drawer for me. Slowly but surely, his became mine, and mine became his. And one day, we signed a lease together.

How do you go from filing a police report to signing a lease together?

I'll tell you manipulation, control, abuse, and loads of dysfunctional and unhealthy encounters.

"Don't stay silent. You have to tell her."

Our words have power. We have to muster the courage to silence the fears and utter the declaration.

Who cares if she's heard you say this a thousand times? Who cares if she doesn't believe you? You need this.

Here goes nothing…

"I have to leave him… I am going to leave him."

She smiled softly and waited for me to continue. I didn't know if meeting with my friend would change anything. She had listened to me profess repeatedly that I was leaving, and she also witnessed me return to this relationship I had emphatically declared I'd never go back to. But she listened intently as I described the latest update on how ugly my relationship had become.

I didn't have much hope.

I tried conveying the mess that had become my life, but I was falling short. How do you unpack the worst three and a half years of your life? Do you say it all? Do you leave some parts out?

I don't know if she will fully get it (I don't think you really do until you live the nightmare).

She listened empathetically, but her occasional pursed lip or furrowed brow didn't hide the confusion and frustration she was feeling. She was following the stories, but she was seeing a disconnect. My words did not do the situation justice. I couldn't adequately paint the picture of the dysfunction and the toxicity.

I'm not sure if I was seeking a listening ear or sound advice. All I knew was that I was running out of options. I needed support. I needed someone to tell me they believed me, and they believed IN me. I didn't know where else to turn or who to talk to. I didn't know what to do.

Then, she asked the question that everyone eventually asked. Its phrasing varies, but the message stays the same.

"Well, why don't you just leave?"

So many thoughts. So many emotions. So many memories. All packed into one seemingly simple question.

She doesn't get it. I seem crazy. I shouldn't have tried.

I dissected her reply word by word.

I hear her saying, "*Well*, why don't you just leave?" as in "Come on now. I see the solution here."

She says, "*Well*" so matter-of-factly as if to say, "A + B = C. This is simple logic, and leaving is the simple answer."

I hear, "Well, why don't you *just leave*?" Like, "Why haven't you thought of this already? It's a no-brainer. It's easy, Courtney. Just do it."

I truly and deeply despise that question. You probably do too.

I can't *just* pack a bag and leave. I can't *just* text him and say, "I'm not coming back."

That's not how it works. And the thing is, he also knows that's not how it works.

I know she means well. She wants the best for me, and she's tired of me telling her the same story on a different day. Same saga, but a different episode. She's tired of watching someone treat me so poorly. She's tired of seeing me settle. She doesn't want to see me belittled anymore. She doesn't want me to have to file another report.

But there's nothing easy about leaving. Yes, I had thought about leaving for good, but it was not that simple. I didn't know how to do it. I always reverted. I always believed in him again. I always gave in.

I wracked my brain to deliver an answer that would satisfy her question. How do I adequately communicate my reasoning without sounding naive, ignorant, or, worse yet, crazy? I began to speak, but all I could muster were half sentences. I couldn't finish a thought.

Processing a minutia of manipulation is paralyzing, to say the least.

Do I even fully understand why I'm staying?

So many thoughts. So many emotions. So many memories.

I tried once more and sadly answered, "It wasn't always like this."

I used to believe my opinion mattered. I used to believe my dreams were of value. I used to feel cherished and pursued. I used to feel safe and secure.

I used to envision our future together. We were happy. We would have gotten married. We would have had kids.

So, *How did I end up here? How did I not see this?*

I couldn't pinpoint one exact moment when our relationship began to derail. There wasn't one particular conversation or event that I could remember. I'm not sure where we got off track or how it got so bad.

I believe, for us, it was the slow fade. The good gradually eroded, and the thrill stalled. Excitement was exchanged for anxiousness. No longer did I look forward to seeing him; instead, I began ducking for cover whenever I sensed him coming.

I didn't know it at the time, but these initial hesitations were warning signs. In the domestic violence arena, they refer to the warnings as flags. Just like stop lights, green is good and means go. Yellow is a warning, and you may not want to proceed. Red is stop! Do not enter! Recognizing yellow and red flags is vital to your safety and the health of any relationship. Stopthehurt.org outlines the

It wasn't always like this

19

differences between yellow and red flags in relationships.

I was ignorant of the warning signs. I got accustomed to the demands. I overlooked the harsh and degrading comments and rolled my eyes when his eyes strayed. Opportunities for inter-action became burdens I begrudgingly endured, and in many cases, my dreams were destroyed by deceit.

And then the stakes are raised.

Your freedom is infringed upon. Your desires are dismantled. And your worthiness is unraveled.

It becomes about survival.

Many of my mantras sounded something like this…

Ignore the insensitive comments.

Brave the mornings and get out of the house.

Avoid people and get through the day.

Stomach one more night of arguments.

Survive one more fight.

I plastered on a smile and let everyone see what I wanted them to see. This valedictorian with entrepreneurial promise was just fine. I convinced myself it would work itself out.

Maybe your mantras sound something like this…

Survive one more work day.

Survive one more conversation.

Survive one more practice.

Survive one more class.

Survive one more hour.

Time screeches to a standstill when you're fighting for survival. You're trying not to drown between the dismay and disbelief. It's hard to accept that this is your life, and you tremble thinking about telling someone your reality.

What if they don't get it?

What if they don't believe you?

You're exhausted by the constant defending, justifying, and protecting.

I don't know your exact story, but I want you to hear this. You did not deserve it then, and you do not deserve it now. I am so sorry for what you've endured or are possibly still enduring.

Physically. Verbally. Emotionally. Financially. Psychologically.

The scars are real and raw.

I see you.

You were trying to protect your kids. That workplace destroyed you. There was no winning with that coach. That one-sided friendship tore you apart. That person dismantled your peace and stole your safety. That divorce broke you.

Whatever the specifics, I see you. You are not alone.

We weren't actively seeking a soul-crushing, manipulative, and controlling relationship. No one actively pursues a relationship, job, or friendship that steals their oxygen supply. Yet, I would venture to say most of us have experienced one, if not all, of these. I personally have experienced quite a few.

Why does this keep happening? Am I too trusting? Am I an easy target? What is it about me that attracts unhealthy, toxic people?

Somehow, I got out. Some might say it was by happenstance, luck, coincidence, a dare, or the stars aligned, but the freedom

I received stemmed elsewhere. Ultimately, my mom's prayers and intercessions came to fruition.

Leaving was hard. Leaving was scary. Leaving, while it was totally worth it, didn't change everything except my address.

I left, but what was I left with?

I was left on the other side of the relationship, trying to understand *how*, *when*, and *why*. It was frustrating and irritating. It was disheartening and even alarming. The loops of memories didn't make sense. They didn't add up.

I couldn't force the memories to make sense. I couldn't control the past, and I couldn't make him care. So at the beginning of my healing, I sat frustrated, irritated, and hurt, hesitantly wondering, "Will I ever recover?"

And to that person who *is* still in that place, still rehearsing that mantra, I see you. I can't suggest you leave. I can't tell you how to leave or when to leave. You don't need to explain yourself to me or anyone else for that matter. This book isn't a how-to on leaving, and this book isn't one to shame or guilt trip you for staying either. You have your reasons for staying. I had mine too.

It was the hardest, most challenging, and most daunting endeavor for me to leave my unhealthy relationship. It took me a little over three years to fully commit to my decision.

I left more than just a relationship. I left behind friends, possessions, and memories. I packed up and moved from my home. I said goodbye to the comforting familiarity of our life together. We had a routine, system, bills, and furniture. And no matter how dysfunctional it was, it was familiar, and the unknown seemed scarier than the toxicity.

Ultimately, I had to choose to remove myself from that sickening security. I had to release the wish that the good would return. I walked away from an old me.

Looking back, I don't recognize that girl anymore. After that relationship ended, I vowed not to lose myself to another relationship. I don't want to passively accept belligerent, degrading, or sarcastic comments in order to keep the peace. I don't want to ignore the tension when my boundaries are bombarded.

When I'm not intentional about protecting those personal boundaries to keep me emotionally healthy and safe, I have looked up and thought, "Dang it. It happened again." I have to assess a relationship. Reestablish a boundary... or two... or five... Or I have to sever the relational tie.

This hasn't happened to me just once. It has happened multiple times. And I thought, "It must be me. I am the common denominator here. There is something about me that is fundamentally screwed up that I keep ending up in these messes."

Maybe you feel that too.

But maybe it's not about us at all. Perhaps it's about something deeper, more deceptive and cunning than we could have ever imagined. Maybe it's the doing of the darkness.

"

But maybe it's not about us at all. Perhaps it's about something deeper, more deceptive and cunning than we could have ever imagined. Maybe it's the doing of the darkness.

"

We are made for relationships, and we know relationships can be messy. But I'm done feeling like a mess and being left with a mess when a relationship ends. I will do life with people, but I won't be sucked into the cyclone of relationship drama, damage, and decay.

On the other side of this book, I pray you emerge a more healed, peaceful, and thriving person. You will thank your previous self for protecting you and getting you this far, and you will embrace the current you who is living in freedom and forgiveness.

Your relationships will prosper. You will exude joy. Thanksgiving will flow from your lips, and your life will shine a path for those seeking the same healing.

People will approach you in wonder and awe. Some will know your past and be confused by your transformation. Some will know your past and desperately desire that exact change. Some will be complete strangers and be drawn to your light.

You will have divine encounters and favored conversations filled with ample opportunity to proclaim the goodness of the Lord. Your testimony will be a beacon for those who are living your past. It will forge a path for those who are trying to climb out of the confusion and heal from the dysfunction.

People will leave your presence knowing God's healing power. They will witness it in your life and embark on a journey to experience it for themselves.

When someone asks you, "How are your relationships so fulfilling? So life-giving? So peaceful, wonderful, and joyful?"

You can authentically and humbly say, "It wasn't always like this."

That moment WILL happen for you. The day I told my friend, "It wasn't always like this," began a healing journey that I am still on, even to this day. When I said I was desperate, ready, and determined for a change, there was no stopping me.

I was desperate to get out. I was ready for a new beginning. I was determined not to give up. Then, I was desperate to heal. I was ready to tackle the hard conversations and determined to unpack the lies.

On this side of my story, when people ask, "Why didn't you leave?" my immediate reaction isn't anger. I'm not annoyed that they don't get it. I don't take offense to their question, and I don't get defensive in my answer.

I see this question as the greatest opportunity to proclaim the Lord's goodness and faithfulness in my life. I am delighted they ask. I am excited to walk them through the hardest and worst years of my life. I look forward to showing them the path of healing I had to endure. I proudly share that I was saved by the grace and mercy of the Lord, and that parts of my story can be described only as, "Because of God…".

Because of God…

— I finally left.

— I had a peace that surpassed all understanding.

— I embraced physical, emotional, and psychological healing.

— I found my identity.

— I began to love myself again.

I pray that through our conversation they walk away with a different perspective when it comes to toxic and abusive relationships. That their understanding is expanded. That their compassion grows. Their awareness is stimulated. Their advocacy for change is challenged. I pray the same thing for you reading this book. If you are in an abusive relationship, on the other side of an abusive relationship, or know someone in an abusive relationship, I pray you approach this book with an openness to explore, grow, and heal.

Ask the hard questions of yourself, your family members, and your friends. Be open to navigating a healing journey that will propel you towards a bright and life-giving future.

While writing this book, I am close to a decade removed from the beginning of that relationship. It's wild to think that years pass whether we actively pursue change or not. I write this book from a place of healing, curiosity, and growth. I am consciously seeking ways to heal from my past. I ask myself hard questions about my thought life, my reactions, and my growth. I still unravel the lies and pursue healthy relationships. I still have to evaluate unhealthy relationships and establish healthy boundaries.

And I am still ever so thankful for the broken me that got me out of that hellacious relationship. I thank God that my current reality does not look like my past. I praise Him that my relationships do not and will never resemble my past.

Saying, "It wasn't always like this," is a testimony in and of itself. It is a reminder of what the Lord brought me out of. It is a testament to the healing work He has done in my life physically, emotionally, and psychologically.

That phrase declares life more abundantly for me, my husband, and my family. It demonstrates the Lord's power to break off generational curses, demolish unhealthy cycles, and crush dysfunction for decades to come.

I am walking in His power and authority that unhealthy, toxic, abusive relationships do not have the final say. They have no hold on our identity. They do not determine our value. They do not take away our worth. They will not make us feel used or embarrassed. They will not leave us isolated or silenced any longer.

You WILL process. You WILL heal. You WILL redeem your future. You WILL rebuild your life.

Pause:

_____

_____

_____

_____

_____

Ponder:

1. What are you hoping to gain from reading this book?

_____

_____

_____

_____

_____

2. Is there someone you'd like to join you on this book-reading journey?

_____

_____

_____

_____

_____

Prayer:

Lord, I pray for my friend embarking on this journey. I pray you shield their heart as they unravel the lies that have been holding them hostage. I pray they stay the course even when emotions are high and the pain feels unrelenting. Revelation 21:4 says, "He will wipe every tear from their eyes. There will be no more death or mourning or crying or pain, for the old order of things has passed away" (New International Version). I pray they begin to believe the old order of things is passing away as they begin to heal, redeem, and rebuild. I pray they bask in your goodness and rely on your comfort, ultimately trusting in the healing process. Amen.

_____

_____

_____

_____

_____

Chapter Two

The Lies That Keep Taking

I laced up my Hoka running shoes, turned on my music, and locked the front door behind me. The fresh and crisp fall morning sent chills (the good kind) down my legs. The sun was peeking over the horizon, illuminating gorgeous strokes of yellow, red, pink, and orange.

New morning, new mercies, am I right? And thank goodness this morning marked a new beginning.

It was foreign going on a run for fun. There was nothing wrong. I was simply pouring back into myself. This starkly contrasts with what I formerly used to run for; I used to run to escape because running is where I felt free. I definitely needed that freedom back when I felt constrained and contained by my life, when there wasn't much living happening at all.

But this was going to be a good run. Controlled breaths filled my lungs as I picked up the pace. I was finding my rhythm again. I exited my neighborhood and started off down the main stretch. When I'm running, I either see nothing or I see everything. I see nothing when I'm in "the zone." In my mind, I'm running so fast (while my app says otherwise), but everything around me is blurred out. It's just me and the road.

When I see everything, I see all of God's beautiful creations from the dew drops on the grass to the quiet buzz of morning traffic. While He didn't create the traffic, I acknowledge He created the people all going different directions in life. On these runs, I reflect on how good God is and how thankful I am to experience this moment.

Whether it's a run where I see nothing or I see everything, I consider this my "me time." My time to release worry and stress. Let them sweat away. My time to let my mind wander into nothingness, into dreams, into possibility. My time to invite creativity in. It was so nice not to need an escape anymore.

I felt the excitement rising. Higher. And higher.

And then I saw the building.

Like a nose dive into frigid and suffocating water, I felt the excitement plummet. My stride morphed into a jog, which then became a crawl. Right there on the city's main street.

No, Courtney. No. Shake it off, sis. You are okay.

You've passed this building a hundred times.

Breathe!

I wanted- no, I *needed* a full breath, but I couldn't. It was trapped behind my past. The street blurred from the welling of tears and mental dizziness. I grabbed my chest in an attempt to slow my heart rate and steady my trembling hands, but to no avail.

It may look like an ordinary building to, but it's so much more in my eyes. It's the building where he humiliated me in front of friends. This is where we had some of our best moments and our worst fights. Where I plastered on a smile and pretended our relationship was fine.

This is the building he abandoned me at with no ride home. The building I walked home from which resulted in a night I never thought I'd survive. This building reminded me that it wasn't just his alcohol consumption that worried me. It reminded me how terrified I was of him and repeating these moments.

No more new morning, new mercies. Thankfulness vanished at the sight of that building. I no longer saw God's creation. All I saw was destruction. So much for feeling freedom because now I needed an escape from my run.

I gently coaxed myself to get back up and keep jogging. I begged my heart to stop sending the worst moments of my life back to the forefront of my memory. Yet, no matter what I tried, the hurricane of emotions overwhelmed me.

My "me time" became an onslaught of destructive thoughts and haunting memories.

No one else will want you.

You are worthless.

No one will believe you.

You are embarrassing.

You can't do anything right.

My prayer interrupted the memories.

"God, I know you are listening. I thought leaving was supposed to solve everything. Why am I still broken?"

I knew God was listening, but I wondered if He actually saw me. Did He see the anguish I was in? Did He understand the frustrating torment I was wrestling with? Did He actually care? And if He did, why was I still reliving the nightmare?

If I'm being honest, this wasn't the first time I had experienced a breakdown since leaving him. Now, admittedly, this was the first time it happened here on the sidewalk and with this particular building, but it wasn't the first breakdown. It wasn't the first time the voices came back, assaulting my new beginning.

Usually, I was good at ignoring the voices, or at a minimum, I got good at accepting them as normal. I got used to hearing those lies said about me. I heard it from him, and then, somewhere along the way, I started saying them to myself. Sometimes, I tried fighting them off, but it feels useless when you try that tactic thousands of times. A waste of energy. I resigned to let the voices stay. But lately, I couldn't simply brush them off. I couldn't whisk the voices away and pretend they didn't exist anymore. They were still affecting me, and the breakdowns were becoming common.

The breakdowns came in various shapes and sizes. Not all were complete meltdowns. Well... Sometimes, they were. Actually... I've had more complete meltdowns than I'd like to admit. Most generally, the breakdowns came from a disconnect like a wiring in my body and brain, that once short-circuited, was now completely fizzled out. Something was definitely breaking down and it came out in the form of my responses, attitudes, and thoughts.

The breakdowns happened right after the relationship separation, but I assumed they would stop on their own simple math. No more him equals no more breakdowns. Sure, they were less frequent as time passed, but it had been years since seeing him. I thought I moved on. I changed jobs and friend groups. I even married the most loving, supportive, and, can I repeat a bazillion times over, *the most patient* man. Yet the breakdowns were still occurring.

Sometimes, it sounded like lashing out at that sweet, patient husband of mine someone who has never demeaned or demoralized me. Someone who has never hit me, let alone has never even raised his voice at me. He is nothing like my past, yet sometimes I treated him like he was responsible for my wounds. Making him pay for my past was not fair.

Other times, the breakdowns looked like me closing myself off from others. People can't hurt you if you're not close to them. Friends can't use your story against you if you never open up.

Goodness, what a somber and lonely life isolation becomes.

Then, there were moments when the breakdowns only involved me and my thoughts. I would lie down for a weekend nap and question my productivity. I would accuse myself of being lazy, or I'd start to cut vegetables and think, "I'm doing this wrong." The breakdowns even followed me to work. I would attend a business meeting agonizing over if I should give my real opinion. Even in the most innocent conversations, I would carefully choose my vocabulary, tone, and inflection as avoid any semblance of tension. I never wanted to repeat that relationship, so I tried everything to avoid anything that sounded like, felt like, and even smelled like the past.

I stopped hanging out with "our" friends. I boycotted restaurants, refused to watch certain movies, and changed my route to work so I wouldn't pass that house. I literally plugged my nose and turned the other way when I smelled that particular cologne and that ever-so-specific brand of cleaning supplies.

The brands. The labels. The buildings. The locations. The people. The music.

It didn't matter where I was, who I was with, or what I was doing. I couldn't escape. Sometimes, I knew the flashback was coming; other times, it was a sneak attack from hell. Sometimes the breakdowns were blinding, and all I could see was my past. The wounds were tender. The memories were too real to deal with. I was living my life based on the lies said about me so many times. The lies were so intricately entangled in my personhood that I couldn't decipher where the lie ended and the truth began.

Other times, I was blinded by the breakdown and didn't see the connection to my past. In those moments, I truly 100% thought the problem was my husband, that restaurant, that phrase, those people. I projected my unresolved pain on anyone in the present even when it was the past that needed to be dealt with. It was whoever or whatever I could blame at that moment because I didn't see the real culprit lurking under the surface.

It's exhausting trying to explore a new me when the old me kept knocking. It's confusing claiming and reclaiming joy and peace over my life yet waking up in a panic. I quote Bible verses day and night and still sweat when I hear their name. Going to church and still feeling empty. So empty. I still jump when the phone rings, and I still hold my breath when I hear the email chime.

Will I ever be able to breathe again?

> **It's exhausting trying to explore a new me when the old me kept knocking.**

Normal, simple, innocent conversations had me second-guessing how to respond. I want to throw my hands in the air. It's maddening!

Why am I still struggling? Why do they still have control? Why do they still get to have control?

I've contemplated giving up, but then they win, and I'm too competitive for that. They've taken too much. They've won too many times. This is supposed to be my time to win.

I circled back to this gnawing notion that he wasn't in my life anymore. I was still battling him, and he didn't even know it. So, was it really him that had control over me, my thoughts, my attitudes, and my responses? I was hesitant to admit it, but the war I was waging was misplaced. I mistakenly attributed the control to a person, but it wasn't a person. The crafty culprit was the lies. The lies were still taking. They were still robbing me of my peace and my security. They continued to tarnish my identity and diminish my value.

Definitions.net describes a lie as "a falsehood uttered or acted for the purpose of deception; an intentional violation of truth."

Wow. Deception and countless violations. Yup, that was precisely my reality.

The lies I believed about myself and my situation were repeatedly spoken over me and to me. Like a self-fulling prophecy, I've heard it so often that it must be true. If they believe this about me, everyone must believe it too. There's no point in trying to change.

These fallacies became realities. They were intentionally woven into my life to squelch the truth. I didn't want to live a life of deception anymore. I didn't want to associate my life with violation. I didn't want to be misled.

I want to walk into the grocery store and not be triggered. I long to listen to music and not worry whether I'll think of him. I want to walk into a public space confidently and not have to quickly scan for his face. I don't want to hide in fear. I don't want to live anxiously from moment to moment.

I want to trust my integrous husband when he says he's texting his guy friends and not become Detective Courtney. I'm not trained to be a detective. It's not in my nature, and it certainly doesn't bring out the good in me. He is exceedingly loyal, yet I keep waiting for him to fail. He repeatedly affirms me and says I'm desirable, but I wonder when he won't want me anymore. When who I am at my core won't satisfy him any longer. I want to believe I am enough just the way I am.

I don't want to question my friends' motives. I want to see the good in them and have faith that they see the good in me. I don't want to secretly worry if they are talking about me behind my back or wonder if they are just my friends out of pity.

I want to believe my boss when he says I'm a valuable team member, and that he's pleased with my work. I don't want to cower when professional boundaries are crossed and stay silent to avoid uncomfortable conversations. I want to handle challenging conversations with dignity and grace.

Unfortunately, you can't do any of that when you're riddled with skepticism and mistrust. You can't give people generous assumptions when you're generally accusatory.

And right now, the truth is I'm sobbing on the sidewalk, remembering all I have lost and thinking, *Will I ever be whole again? Will I ever feel valuable and worthy again? Will I ever find myself again?*

The truth is I'm just not there yet. Maybe you're not there yet, either.

You can't give people generous assumptions when you're generally accusatory.

And that's okay.

But we have to start somewhere. Can we start by acknowledging that we have made progress? You might be thinking, "Yeah, right. Come live a day in my world." And it's true I don't know exactly where you're at in life at this very moment, but I know we all have made progress. It might not be much, but we have—if you look deep enough. Wherever you are... on the couch, in your car, at your desk, or weeping on the sidewalk like myself... we have come so far.

We have to acknowledge that we aren't in that place anymore. We aren't in that season anymore.

But there is more work to be done.

Yuck. Work. Sounds hard.

I initially thought that if I kept myself busy, I wouldn't have to acknowledge what was happening to me and my soul. If I stayed distracted, the lies would be less destructive. But pretending the lies weren't affecting me prevented the healing I desperately needed, which is also hard. I guess I have a choice. I can choose which "hard" I want to deal with. I can put in the hard work and tackle these lies, or I can continue to live a hard life and let the lies run rampant.

So, in the same breath we have to acknowledge that the lies still have a hold on us.

It stinks. It royally stinks.

One lie, multiple lies, or lies you don't even know about yet... it doesn't matter. It all stinks.

But remember, getting to where you are took more than just guts. Chances are that nobody will understand the sacrifices it took to get you here. They won't understand the back-and-forth contemplation, the pros and cons lists, the role-playing of scenarios, the factors and fears, the pleading, the price and the prayers.

But they also won't understand your tenacious, persevering spirit, the ultimate strength and courage you developed, or the desire to believe in and build a better life.

It's okay if they don't understand. I do. And more importantly, God does.

If you are new to the idea of God or are revisiting what you believe about Jesus and faith, let me encourage you.

He does see us, and He does care. He's not intimidated by our doubts and fears. He's not surprised by our outbursts and questioning. It was in my outburst and questioning that the Lord met me on Main Street that particular day, and He can meet you wherever you are too.

It was as if the Lord knelt down beside me on the sidewalk. He stooped down to my level and gently whispered to my soul, *"I have so much in store for you."*

At first, I wasn't sure what that meant, but it instantly calmed my heart. Apparently, whatever He had for me was in abundance since He had "so much." And He did say, "in store." Like whatever *it* was, it was there, ready to go, on the shelf. Ironically, I didn't even ask what *it* was. I was simply intrigued that it could be different from my present reality. I'm pretty sure anything would have been an upgrade from bawling on the concrete for my community to see.

"I have so much in store for you."

66

I have so much in store for you.

99

It made me think of Proverbs 3:9-10, "Honor the Lord with your wealth, with the firstfruits of all your crops; then your barns will be filled to overflowing, and your vats will brim over with new wine" (New International Version).

While these verses are talking about tithing, it reminded me that

38

there is no cap with God. He has no limit. If I simply honor Him with my best (which wasn't looking too great at that moment), He pours out the overflow. He brings in new wine.

My best at that moment was that I was present. I had shown up. I mustered enough energy to sit and listen to what the Lord was saying directly to me and for me. I wish there were more, but that was the best I could offer. He wasn't judging.

The overflow sounded amazing, but I whispered, deflated, "Lord, I've been running on empty. If I could just be full again, I'd be satisfied."

He echoed, *"I have so much in store for you."*

I felt something different rising this time. Hope.

He didn't want to just fill me up. He wanted to give me the overflow. He wasn't content with leaving me satisfied. He wasn't okay with getting me back to my old self or my normal state. He wanted to bring in the new, and I realized I also longed for something new.

Are you longing for something new? What would new look like for you?

The Lord has so much in store for you.

Are you hesitating to hope? It's scary. It's unknown. I know for me, hoping has let me down many times. But maybe that's because my hope was misplaced. What if this time it could be different?

You don't have to be satisfied with enduring the triggers and the setbacks. You don't have to be content putting up with the lies and thinking it will be like this forever.

The Lord wants to bring overflow to your life. He wants to bring in the new wine. Something exhilarating. Something good that will last. That's right, good things can last. It doesn't have to end in a repeat like last time. He's inviting us to participate in a wonderful life He has prepared for us. He doesn't want us to merely cooperate. There's no fun or joy or life more abundantly in begrudgingly cooperating. He wants us to experience *all* that He has for us. To be an active participant.

I used the backside of my sleeve to wipe away the tear-stained snot mixture that had become my face. I picked myself up off the pavement. I played it off for the cars passing by like I had been tying my shoe for the better portion of ten minutes. As I stood and brushed myself off, I waved at a few passing cars as if to say, "Nothing to see here random citizens. Keep on movin'. I'm just working on my healing here."

And then I decided… better yet, I declared I would not let the lies keep taking!

I knew it would be a challenge, but it would be possible and, more so, incredibly worth it.

It reminded me of a note my mom wrote in one of my journals.

On the inside cover. she wrote,

"Dear Miss Courtney, I have loved you all of your life. You make me shake my head; you also make me smile. Never doubt for one moment that God doesn't have an amazing plan for your life--not just a mediocre plan that you can tolerate, but one that you cannot fathom--actually knit together with His own hands.

'What do you mean, if I can?' Jesus asked. 'Anything is possible if a person believes.' The father instantly replied, 'I do believe, but help me not to doubt!' Mark 9:23-24

-Mom a/k/a Brendar"

The Lord has loved *you* all of His life. You probably make Him shake His head, but you also make Him smile. He does have an amazing plan for you, and I love what my mom said, "not just a mediocre plan that you can tolerate, but one that you cannot fathom…"

Some of you right now are thinking of all the excuses why you can't journey down this path of healing. Some of you are petrified to acknowledge the lies. Some of you are listing out all the reasons why it won't work for you. You will believe it for others, but you won't believe it for yourself because believing in the past has gotten you where you are today.

You believe you're plagued with bad luck, bad choices, and bad people. If there was an award for the most let-down friendships, broken relationships, and worst work environments, you'd be the all-time winner. You would wear the crown of handling the most dysfunctional family members and going on the most destructive dates.

But guess what? I won't let you discount yourself. Not this time. I won't let others or even yourself dismiss this opportunity for your healing. Believing doesn't have to end in bewilderment. Believing doesn't have to end in a repeat of the past. We can rewrite your history with hope.

And if you're not ready to believe in better, I'll hold onto that hope for you. I'll carry it while you learn to trust again, unpack the lies, and navigate healing. I'll keep presenting the truth and telling you about the ultimate hope we have in Christ. Because as much hope as I can hold for you, the Lord has so much more in store.

He's waiting for you.

The Lord wants the absolute best for you! I want the absolute best for you. It is possible, and we will work through doubt and unbelief. We will remind ourselves of this extraordinary plan

He has for us. And we will expect so much more.

Show up with your questions. Show up with your concerns. Show up with your confusion. But the point is you have to show up!

Come expecting personal discovery and intense healing. Expect rejuvenation and renewal. Expect to come out the other side of this book transformed.

Do it for your friends. Do it for your kids. Do it for your family- present and future. Do it so that generations beyond you will live in the freedom you fought so hard to obtain. Do it for you.

If I haven't been real enough, these next chapters are tough to read. This one was tough, but trust me, it becomes more challenging. They are grueling to sift through, contemplate, and process. They are some of the top lies I believed about myself, my situation, and others in my unhealthy, toxic relationship. You may resonate with them too. For you, it might be a former partner, spouse, boss, or coach. Or it might be an estranged family member or friend. I don't know your exact situation, but you've been thinking about that person since you picked up this book.

For some of you, that person is removed from your life; for others, you're in the thick of it now. Whatever the case, acknowledging the lies still have a hold on you is the first step in healing and reclaiming your value and identity. It's challenging to tackle the lies that have held you in bondage for so long, and each of us battles different lies. Some are playing on a recurring loop in our heads. Others come and go with the seasons, times and places we venture. But they don't get a free ride anymore. It's time to identify and understand what specific lies you still believe and how they control you. Where are they showing up in your life? How are they showing up in your life? Then the most liberating moment occurs when we learn how we combat them to live a promised abundant life.

Let me tell you from experience, that you will be able to breathe again, and you will find yourself again.

I don't know about you, but I'm not settling for mediocrity. I'm not okay with a life I'll have to tolerate. I want to live life more abundantly. I desire the overflow. I desire the new wine. If that is also the desire of your heart, let's get started.

Pause:

_____

_____

_____

_____

_____

Ponder:

1. Do you know what lies have a hold on you? If so, what are they?

_____

_____

_____

_____

_____

2. Have you experienced a sidewalk moment in your life? What did the Lord speak to you at that time?

_____

_____

_____

_____

_____

Prayer:

Lord, I pray that as memories surface they surrender them to you. I pray they find the courage to dig deeper and find life more abundantly. I pray they will not settle until they find the new wine the overflow. And according to Psalm 37:4 I pray as they delight in You, that You reveal the desires of their heart. Amen.

_____

_____

_____

_____

_____

Chapter Three

Massively Manipulated

Manipulation is a destructive art accomplished through ordinary conversation and seemingly innocent remarks. I didn't even realize I was being manipulated. My words were used against me, and my intentions were twisted. When I confronted him, he was shocked, baffled, and even hurt that I would accuse him of something so incredulous.

His memory of that night and mine couldn't have been more different.

At first, I was stunned. I couldn't move. I felt something drop onto my hand. And then more drops followed. I stuck my hand under the porch light. My hand was covered in blood.

Drop by drop, my hand filled up. I shook my hand towards the grass, begging the blood to leave. But again, drop by drop, my hand filled.

Then I noticed the pain. My lip was throbbing, and my head was spinning. I placed my hands on the siding of the house to steady myself. I opened my eyes wide and rolled them around, willing the stars to disappear, but blotches of light continued to flicker in and out of my vision. Then I realized he was gone. He didn't stick around. He simply vanished into the darkness of night.

As I slowly walked back into the house, cupping my chin from the dripping blood, the once lively party came to a stand-still. The music stopped. The voices were silenced. The discomfort was palpable. One by one, the guests were ushered out. There wasn't a need to explain what had happened. Everyone understood.

As I was taken home by a friend, I sat in the passenger seat rocking in disbelief.

Why would he do that?

This shouldn't have happened.

It was just because he was drunk.

He didn't mean it. He loves me.

"Courtney, this isn't love. My love will never hurt you."

The Lord was still beckoning me. Even in my worst moment, He was inviting me back to Him. I couldn't bear it. I didn't want to come to terms with how my life was turning out. I didn't want to face the Lord broken, bruised, and ashamed.

He hit me.

My brain wouldn't process the words. They were so foreign to me.

HE hit me.

He HIT me.

He hit ME!

The sentence looped inside my brain. Each syllable wrecked me as I tried to understand the events of that evening. As if this night wasn't shocking enough, I wasn't prepared for what was to come the next day, the next week, and the following months.

His version- When I reached for his shoulder, he shrugged me off and left the party.

My version- When I reached for his shoulder, he backhanded me and left me at the party.

His version was revised- He never hit me.

My version- He backhanded me so hard, that a dentist had to use muscle stem therapy on my jaw to correct the damage inflicted.

His version was revised again- He never even touched me.

My version- He backhanded me so hard I cried every time I brushed my teeth for the next few weeks due to the bruising.

His version was revised again- He was too drunk to remember anything, so he can't apologize for something he doesn't remember. Also, there were no witnesses, so who says there's anything to apologize for?

My version- Again, look at my face! My protruding cheek. My swollen bottom lip, which, when pulled back, exposed the purple, blue, and green bruises. I would say that is worth apologizing for.

His version conclusion- According to his therapist, I always bring out the worst in him when drinking. So, he can still drink, but I cannot be around him when he drinks.

My version conclusion- Excuse me? Say what?

I questioned whether the chain of events happened the way I remembered, and sometimes, I questioned whether the event occurred.

I sought out help from mutual friends. Many told me they wanted to stay out of it. Or they were his friends first, so asking for their support was unreasonable. Or the best response yet was not even receiving a reply.

I was distanced from my closest friends and family to ensure the survival of this toxic relationship. Bruised and bewildered, all I could think was, *I'm the problem. The problem is me.*

The truth was, I wasn't the problem. The problem was that I was dealing with a narcissistic abuser, and I found out too late.

Eleanor D. Payson wrote a phenomenal book, *The Wizard of Oz and Other Narcissists.* She describes narcissism as self-worship. His charm lured me in. His confidence was admirable, but it was a facade. Narcissists, whether overt or covert, need to "manipulate people in order to maintain an endless supply of attention, control, status, money, power or recognition."

If your repertoire of external dialogue and internal thoughts commonly includes:

"You're right, it's my fault."

"I'm so sorry. Please forgive me."

"Am I going crazy?"

"Maybe I'm being dramatic."

"Did it really happen?"

"You are responsible for this."

"Nobody believes you."

"Nobody will believe you."

"No one else will love you."

You have probably been manipulated, and if you are concerned you're dealing with a narcissist, please review the list of questions Payson provides in her first chapter.

Manipulators are the king (or queen) of the castle. What they say goes. They call the shots. They make the demands. Psychology Today says, "Manipulators deliberately create an imbalance of power and exploit the victim to serve his or her agenda."

Your role is to get in line or get out. But the rulers of the castle are much too smart to boldly claim their title as manipulators. Instead, they have engineered tactics to produce compliance.

Their tactics look like but are not limited to—guilt trips, playing the victim, stonewalling, gaslighting, blame-shifting, exploiting weaknesses, and isolation.

Guilt trip- Have you ever been told you don't care enough? You don't love them enough? If roles were reversed, they would do it for you. They would *absolutely* reciprocate, but they aren't in a position to do so right now. Then they shock you with this response, "You understand, right?"

They would buy you that car. They would pay for that trip. They would help you with that errand. But do you return the favor? No. You're too selfish. You're entitled and self-preserving. How could you do this to them?

Aren't you a Christian? I don't think this is what Jesus would do. Do you even care about this ministry?

Basically, sell your soul for their sake. Their cause is your cause.

And if you disagree, well there is something fundamentally wrong with you, and they will be the first to let you know and continually remind you of your fundamental flaw.

Playing the victim- Nothing is ever their fault. It's not their fault that they are the way they are. It's because of their past: their past relationship, job, family, etc. Anything to deflect responsibility for their actions. They need sympathy.

They have nowhere to go no one to turn to. If you leave them now, they will harm themselves. They might even threaten to attempt suicide. They need you and can't live without you. If you really loved them, you would stay.

Or they assert that they are upset you keep "attacking" them by bringing up the past. You are the unforgiving one because you can't let things go. It hurts them to talk about those things, and it's cruel that you would even make mention of it.

P.S. Remember why you keep bringing it up? Because you've never found closure from the first incident! Why? Because they keep denying responsibility, guilt-tripping you, and/or playing the victim.

Stonewalling- You've never played the quiet game quite like this before. Their silence is deafening.

There is no discussion to be had. They will not listen to you. In fact, they don't even hear you. They refuse to make eye contact with you or acknowledge your presence. You are a waste of space and an inconvenience of their breath.

They are made of stone and you will not penetrate this wall of defense they have constructed. They will be in control if and when we discuss this topic, and right now, they refuse.

Gaslighting- The purpose of gaslighting is to obstruct and distort what you believe is reality. They essentially rewrite history. They will change details or completely deny that an event ever took place. They will invalidate, diminish, and ignore your needs. This leaves you feeling crazy.

They also describe you to you and others as if you were crazy. They've perfected the inquisitive yet equally judgmental look that says "Wow, did you really just say that?" Or the sympathetic side frowns which states, "You poor thing. I'll take over the conversation from here." And don't forget, they've mastered the never-ending eye-rolling and the exaggerated and exasperated sighs.

You replay the scenario. You rehearse what was said and what was done. You were there. It is time-stamped on your phone. The video was taken. The pictures were captured. It was written in your journal. How can they say it never happened?

He repeatedly told me that he either did not hit me or it didn't happen like I said it did, and I actually started to believe it. My face was swollen. My lip was bruised. I had dental appointments and therapy sessions. Yet, somehow, I started to believe he didn't hit me.

Blame-shifting- This tactic occurs when they turn the focus off of themselves and point the finger at someone else, which usually turns out to be you. There is no way it could be their fault. They cannot admit wrongdoing because they would have to be accountable for their actions.

In the weeks and months following the incident I shared, he would remind me that I was partly to blame because I followed him outside. I brought this upon myself because I should have known he was not in a good mood. I started to believe I deserved this treatment.

I apparently was also to blame for my "mental issues" following the incident. I panicked when I saw a first responder. I froze when I heard their sirens. When someone knocked on my door, I jumped. The nightmares wouldn't cease. I was told it was my fault I called the police in the first place so I could deal with the aftermath.

According to the National Center for PTSD, "Posttraumatic Stress Disorder is an anxiety disorder that can occur following the experience or witnessing of a traumatic event. A traumatic event is a life-threatening event such as military combat, natural disasters, terrorist incidents, serious accidents, or physical or sexual assault in adult or childhood."

PTSD has a variety of symptoms, but I specifically experienced the following:

I replayed the incident over and over again.

I was constantly on guard and skittish.

I felt emotionally numb and detached.

I experienced waves of intense emotions like: sadness, fear, despair, guilt, and self-hatred.

I could not imagine life beyond the situation. There was no hope for me or a future.

I wasn't at fault, and I shouldn't have been blamed. It was a serious condition that I needed licensed help to heal. But this was yet another tactic to use my vulnerabilities against me.

Exploiting weaknesses- You don't have it all together. You are inherently flawed. There is so much wrong with you. You don't do this right. You can never do this correctly.

Remember those vulnerable moments when you shared your deepest desires? When you were transparent with your struggles? When you confided in them about your past? All, and I mean ALL of those conversations, are fair game to be used... against you.

If I asked for help, I was either too needy, or he would tell me to figure it out myself.

Other times, he would use my age against me. If he thought I should know the answer or be able to do the task he would sarcastically judge, "How old are you again?" If he didn't think my opinion was valid, he would say I was too young to know anything, or inexperienced to voice my thoughts. If I displayed interest in something he thought was beneath me, he'd exclaim, "Act your age! You're so embarrassing." My age was consistently used to undermine my thoughts and actions.

Exploiters will constantly remind you of your shortcomings in order to belittle, demean, or silence you. They will flaunt your weaknesses to showcase their superiority. It gives them the upper hand and sends you shrinking back in humiliation and passivity.

They are cruel in private hurling insults and rehearsing your past mistakes. You would think that in public, you'd find a reprieve, but they are even more cunning in this arena. They casually compliment another person by saying they wish you were more like them. Around others they criticize the way you eat, speak, and drink. They elaborately and enthusiastically tell stories that paint you as the buffoon, the screw-up, and the ultimate butt of the joke. Even if these examples weren't weaknesses prior to your relationship with them, you surely feel inadequate now.

Isolation- Isolation is massively manipulative. You can be isolated physically, kept at a distance, or cut off entirely from your support system. Why do you need family or friends when you have them? They want you to believe they are your source for everything so no one else can matter. No one can encroach upon the territorial hold. They begin to control your time, friendships, spiritual guidance and/or resources. They convince you that they need to be the sole person influencing you in every area of your life. Everyone else's influence is on par with garbage.

You can be isolated psychologically. Whether they are things said directly to you or things you come to believe, these phrases and thoughts isolate.

"You are the only one who believes this."

"No one else is going through this."

"Nobody will believe you."

"You are all alone."

"If you do/don't do this, I'll keep the kids from you."

You can even be isolated financially. Your source of income and/or livelihood funnel through one outlet–usually the person manipulating you. If you don't comply with their wishes or their regulations, then you don't get to pay the electric bill. You don't get to send money with your kids (and yes, sometimes these kids are THE MANIPULATOR'S kids too) for school lunches. You don't get to buy groceries that day, week, or month.

I recognize that some of my readers may be thinking, "They should just go out and get a job so they can have the finances they need.

Unfortunately, "should be able to" and "are allowed to" aren't necessarily congruent in many manipulative relationships.

What happens when the manipulator has all the paychecks automatically deposited to the joint checking account that is actually just their checking? Or after every shift, they demand cash from their partner? And if the partner doesn't willingly give the cash up, or heaven forbid, tries to withhold some of the cash, there are consequences. Sometimes these consequences are physical repercussions to the partner, their children, or even to their pets. What if the abuser takes out credit cards in the victim's name, or they cosign a loan together? Or what if the abuser is a family member, pastor, or boss who heavily influences where they spend and invest their money? They might be coerced to enable a codependent sibling because family helps the family. Or you HAVE to give to this ministry/charity (one they chose or support) or else you're a bad person and don't truly care about others. Some might even question if you have true faith.

Similar to the fact that domestic violence can happen to anyone, the same applies to abusers. An abuser comes from anywhere and can have any background. An abuser on the outside looks like a friend, a pastor, a coworker, etc. (2019, "Signs of abuse" section, para 1). An abuser's identification does not come from their title, position, or job. Rather, an abuser's identification comes from a pattern of characteristics because abuse does not have as much to do with their outward appearance or resume as it does with the condition of their heart and mind.

Some of these scenarios may sound far-fetched and even ridiculous. But these aren't just scenarios. These are real-life examples of financial manipulation at its finest. The victims believe they are trapped financially, tied to their manipulator, and thus dependent on them.

I'm not trying to make up excuses for those of us who have stayed in seriously unhealthy relationships, I am, however, trying to educate others on the reality and seriousness of many people stuck in manipulative, abusive relationships. The dynamics and intricacies of the lies go deeper than what we see on the surface.

> 66
>
> *It's a game where the rules keep changing, but you always lose.*
>
> 99

No one wakes up one morning and

says, "I can't wait to be manipulated today!" It's an absurd statement, but so many of us find ourselves being manipulated. It's a game where the rules keep changing, but you always lose. And let me tell you, I kept losing!

What Manipulation Caused Me To Believe

Here are some examples of the self-talk I formed after being manipulated for so long:

— I can only give my opinion if it matches theirs. Otherwise, be prepared for a fight, which will result in me agreeing with their opinion to keep the peace.

— Be prepared to always say sorry and ask for forgiveness even if they are clearly in the wrong.

— I don't have my own feelings and emotions. I must mirror theirs.

— I should always sacrifice my goals to support theirs.

— Dreaming is not for me. I won't amount to anything.

— I am responsible for their actions.

— I caused their outbursts. Whether sober orintoxicated, never rock the boat.

— I am replaceable. Shape up, or he'll have a new you by tomorrow.

Manipulation caused me to believe that if there was a problem, it was me.

— I'm so selfish. I only think about myself.

— I've lived a sheltered life. I don't really know how the world works.

Manipulation caused me to believe that if there was a problem, it was me. It was always me. Which further confirmed to me that there was something intrinsically wrong with me. The manipulation game left me believing I was responsible for other people's actions and reactions. It was a never-ending battle to do the right thing and say the right thing.

It was exhausting to accommodate him, justify my actions, and defend our relationship to others. It became "easier" to cater to his wants, preferences, and desires. I say "easier" because it was a battle anytime I didn't align with him. If I didn't agree or comply, there was no discussion. He'd pick which tactic suited his fancy for that particular moment, and by the end of the battle, I had lost yet again.

At some point, you just don't want to fight anymore. You've been dismantled of your armor. You've been relentlessly beaten down. For some of us, it's verbal; for others it's physical, psychological, or financial. And for many of us, it's all of the above.

So, yes, it was easier at the moment to just comply. I expended less energy. But each time I complied, I lost more of myself. I began to deteriorate as I continued apologizing, covering, and caving.

❝ *According to The National Domestic Violence Hotline, "On average, a woman will leave an abusive relationship seven times before she leaves for good."* **❞**

I believed anything I said, did, or touched was tainted by my inadequacy. I was wrong constantly, while no one else could do anything wrong. At times, I felt lucky to have him in my life because he was supposedly helping me. He was weeding out the parts of me that were too immature, dramatic, and naive.

57

Author Brendon Burchard says, "When someone disrespects you, beware the impulse to win their respect. For disrespect is not a valuation of your worth but a signal of their character." I had been disrespected, to say the least, but I kept returning to him trying to win his respect.

According to The National Domestic Violence Hotline, "On average, a woman will leave an abusive relationship seven times before she leaves for good."

Seven times.

Unfortunately, I am proof that this particular statistic is accurate.

I just wanted him to see something in me. I wanted his approval so badly. I let him speak into my life and tell me what was true for me. I let him dictate what my reality was. I believed I was the bad influence. I believed I caused his harsh and violent outbursts.

I was responsible for him locking me in the bathroom. I was to blame when he punched the bathroom door in a fit of anger. It was my fault he was over-the-top angry and kicked in the stairwell and splintered another door.

Over the course of three years, I rationalized with myself, saying...

He hasn't hit me in over a year so we are better.

He hasn't cussed me out in a month so we are making progress.

He hasn't made a degrading, devaluing comment about me this past week so he is improving.

He didn't come home sloppy drunk last night, so maybe he's not an alcoholic anymore?

Or the one I clung to the most... *I know the real him. I see his potential. I just need to hang in there so he can be the man I know he truly is, and we can have the amazing life I know we should have.*

All of these were lies I had convinced myself.

It took me too long to realize it wasn't my character or my personhood that should have been in question. I had to come to the end of myself to understand I was being manipulated, and it felt like a devastating defeat to admit I was not okay. And that this relationship was far from okay.

Pause:

_____

_____

_____

_____

_____

Ponder:

1. How do you know when someone is treating you poorly? How do you react/respond when someone treats you poorly?

_____

_____

_____

_____

_____

2. In a current or former relationship, have you been on the receiving end of any of the tactics mentioned? Have you knowingly or unknowingly used these tactics against someone else?

_____

_____

_____

_____

_____

Prayer:

Lord, I pray you would pierce through the chaos of manipulation. Give my friend clarity to see how they are treated in their relationships and how they, in turn, treat others. I pray you give them the confidence to confide in you with everything they have been dealing with. Illuminate the tactics that have been used against them and are still being used against them. I pray in alignment with Isaiah 54:17 for a hedge of protection over their heart and mind that no weapon of deception or manipulation will prosper against them anymore! Amen!

_____

_____

_____

_____

_____

Chapter Four

Paralyzed by Fear

Think of the scariest time in your life. Where were you? What day was it? Who was with you?

Did you think you would survive?

I didn't.

I'm almost ten years removed from this incident, but I still get sick to my stomach remembering it. It's not as raw and as painful, but it still makes me cringe. The memory still stings.

It still makes me wrap my arms around myself in a tight hug, slowly rocking, trying to console that vulnerable and terrified younger me.

The scariest night of my life was in a dark alley behind the pink house. I didn't think he would ever let me leave. It didn't matter how much I begged. It didn't matter how much I cried. I was at his mercy.

I can still smell the crisp air filling my nostrils. I can still feel the cool breeze brushing my cheeks. I can also still remember the adrenaline coursing through my veins. I still sense the panic gripping my chest.

He kicked my purse across the alley, strewing the contents in the dirt and gravel. He picked up my purse again and shook out the remaining items, hoping my keys would be lost in the debris.

He threatened. He yelled. He chased.

I pleaded and begged. I apologized.

Lastly, I threatened, "I'm going to call the cops!"

His response was, "Go ahead, call the cops. You saw how that worked out last time. You'll probably get arrested before me."

I was speechless, frozen in place.

He was right. The last time I called the police, the system let me down. Why should I try again?

So instead, I gave up. I surrendered and prayed I'd make it to see tomorrow.

...

Yes, I know I didn't give you every detail of that night. I understand I didn't connect all the dots for you. Thankfully, I did make it to see tomorrow.

You don't need to know every time I was cussed out. Or every time I was cheated on. Or every time I was humiliated, taunted, or threatened. You don't need the account of every time

I begged for affection and love– or the times it was forced upon me. You don't need the details of when my head was slammed, my body bruised, or my mind warped. You don't need the proof of the times I was locked out... or locked in.

You don't need them because you've lived them. Or, at the very least, someone you know and love has lived them. I'm sure you or your loved one has lived and relived the worst nights of your life. The memory loops that cannot be erased. The fear that lingers behind the front door.

You've heard the slammed doors and cabinets. You've witnessed the doors, the glasses, the lamps, and the frames be smashed.

You watched them aggressively pour out bottle after bottle, yelling, "Is this what you want?! Are you happy now?!" And in theatrical fashion, they shatter the glass all over the floor.

You've experienced the fear consuming your body. Your throat constricting. Your chest heaving. The nausea rising. Your body trembling. Your hands still shaking even after the threat has passed.

Bruises.

Blood.

Broken bones.

You brace yourself for the beatings–mentally and physically.

And even when the destruction wasn't directly aimed at you, the message was still clear.

Be thankful it was the door and not you.

This time, it was the railing, next time it could be your face.

Every time you pass the smashed-in door, the splintered railing, or the spot where the lamp used to sit, you remember what they were capable of in their rage. You are reminded of who you're up against if you dare.

And God forbid someone asks you about your bruises. Or someone comments on how your partner spoke to you. You suddenly become the ultimate denier. Fear makes you lie for them! In a feeble attempt to remain in their good graces, you think if you cover for them, maybe they will appreciate you or see the effort you are putting into your relationship.

Can't they see that you love and care for them so much that you are willing to forget about this incident and not let a soul know? That you will sacrifice for them? Again?

Maybe, just maybe, they'll finally see you. Instead, you find yourself even more entrenched in the terrifying web of their control.

They have woven fear into every fiber of your being. Your natural reaction is to tense up when someone approaches or wince at the connection of physical touch. No one is safe. You're always guarded, your fight/flight/freeze response on standby.

Isn't it crazy that fear is a part of the human experience? And in small doses, fear can be healthy! Fear alerts us when something is wrong, something is off, or something is dangerous. Fear can arise when trying something new or outside of our comfort zone, but fear in large doses for extended periods can be crippling and subsequently traumatizing.

These relationships become about survival.

When you're in an abusive relationship, fear consumes you. You wake up fearing the day. Throughout the day, you look over your shoulder and calculate every word and action. You constantly check your phone because you have to reply immediately no matter what, no matter when. Then, at night, you go to sleep dreading tomorrow. These relationships become about survival.

I have experienced this paralyzing fear in three scenarios.

1. The Fear while in the relationship

2. The Fear of leaving the relationship

3. The Fear on the other side of the relationship

Let's unpack these scenarios shall we? These explanations are not an end-all-be-all. They might not cover every aspect of toxic, unhealthy, abusive relationships, but these are some of the most common scenarios I've personally dealt with and have heard others experience.

1.   The Fear while in the relationship

Everything you have read up to this point in this chapter has explored the fear individuals experience while in a relationship. Most people don't understand why others get into these types of relationships in the first place. Others may give them the benefit of the doubt and understand the powers of manipulation (see previous chapter), but people on the outside don't understand why they would stay in that type of relationship.

In order to comprehend this concept, we must understand how classical conditioning and learned helplessness works.

In the 60's, Dr. Martin Seligman conducted a research experiment on dogs.

This is sad. You have been warned.

Seligman would ring a bell and then shock the dog. He repeated this over and over again, and the dogs associated the bell ringing with a shock. Even when Seligman rang the bell and did NOT shock the dogs, they behaved as if they had been shocked. They knew that bell meant pain.

The experiment went further when Seligman put these dogs into a crate. The flooring on half of the crate was electrified, and the other half of the crate was not. There was a very small divide between the two areas that the dog could easily jump over. So, in theory, when the dog (on the electrified side) felt the shock, he should simply jump to the non-electrified side.

Guess what the dogs did when shocked?

They laid down.

They lay down and endured the abuse.

This condition was coined "learned helplessness." From the bell ringing and the shock being administered, the dogs transferred that knowledge into the crate. They reasoned they had no escape from the pain. They assumed they were helpless and there was no reprieve from or remedy for the abuse. It was coined "learned" helplessness because Seligman continued his research and tried the crate portion of the experiment on dogs who had not been previously shocked after the bell rang.

Guess what those dogs did when shocked?

> **The more people are beaten down physically, emotionally, psychologically, etc., the more we learn to lie down. We begin to believe the lies...**

They hopped to the other side of the crate! They knew there was a way out! Or even if they didn't know there was a way out, they were willing to try and remove themselves from the harm.

Are you seeing the correlation here between the dogs and abusive relationships? The more people are beaten down physically, emotionally, psychologically, etc., the more we learn to lie down. We begin to believe the lies…

This is the best I can do.

I'm not worth anything.

I deserve to be treated this way.

This is as good as life gets.

And on and on and on. We keep getting shocked, and we keep lying down.

We are trapped. We are stuck. We are powerless.

Life becomes about survival, and fear overrides the option to jump to the other side.

2.   The Fear of leaving the relationship

Why would someone stay in a relationship that is terrifying? Why didn't they jump to the other side of the proverbial crate before they were shocked into submission? The first few shocks should have been an indication to run away, right?

Great question and good point! I'm glad you asked. An abuser's goal is to retain power and control. Please review the Power and Control Wheel on page 73, and remember that while some of the verbiage is directed towards men, women can be abusers as well. And if you'd like a further explanation of the Power and Control wheel, please use the URL below to watch the two-minute video. https://youtu.be/5OrAdC6ySiY

This wheel is geared towards people in intimate partner relationships, but you might also find similar power and control dynamics in any familial relationship, job situation, or even in the church world.

The Power and Control Wheel reveals the top reasons victims stay, and here are a few more:

-The fear in this relationship is not as terrifying as what could be on the other side of leaving the relationship. At least I know what to expect from them. What if it's worse without them? This relationship, as awful as it is, is known. I have become comfortable with this toxicity. Basically, I will endure my current situation because I am more afraid of what it looks like to leave this relationship.

-Soul ties. Whoowee, this is a biggin'. We will discuss this in another chapter. But with the mention of soul ties, let's throw in spiritual commitments. For some people, the person abusing them is their spouse, fiancé, or intimate partner. If you've grown up with any spiritual practice in your life, most generally that community promotes longevity and commitment in the relationship. We think that if we have married or even committed to marrying someone, it justifies the abuse we are enduring. If we are dating, we think getting engaged will solve our problems. Or if we are engaged, when we get married, things will calm down. Or if we are married, let's start a family to create peace.

I grew up in a Christian church, and this was my personal struggle. I was physically intimate with this person, and I thought I needed to stick it out to undo the wrongful sin I had committed. If we just get married, it will justify the fact that we had premarital sex. Or I would think I cannot give up on them—the Lord never gave up on me. I'm committed and devoted.

Some people will stay in the relationship because their pastor told them divorce would be worse… I'm going to just assume here, with the biggest generous assumption I can, that particular pastor has not suffered through an abusive relationship. Because if they had, they certainly would not tell someone that divorce is not allowed, so stay with the abuser to honor God.

Knowing what I know now about the Lord and my relationship with Him, He does not call us to sacrifice our safety for the sake of abuse. He would not ask us to endure unhealthy, toxic relationships no matter who it involves.

-Well, I know _____ (insert the person's name who has the worst relationship you know of) has it way worse than I do. I shouldn't be complaining. I can suck it up. Friend, just because you believe that so and so has it worse than you do, that does not mean you should also stomach suffering. The cycle has to stop.

-I'm not being hit, so is it really that bad? Yes friend, it is. I've been on the other side of some brutal beatings with just verbiage. The *Journal of Family Violence* conducted research on women specifically and how it related to their self-esteem, discovering that "when compared to physical, sexual, or other forms of intimate partner violence, psychological abuse that is controlling, restricting, degrading, isolating, or dominating in nature prove to have the most debilitating effects upon the self-esteem of battered women" (Lin-Roark, Church, & McCubbin, 2015, p. 202).

It hurts. It scars. It creates fear. And yes, it is really that bad. You cannot compare your suffering or your abuse to someone else's. If they are violating your boundaries and not respecting you as a human being, then that relationship is below par.

> **The cycle has to stop.**

-Stalking is yet another reason victims stay. According to www.stalkingawareness.org, 40% of stalking victims are stalked by a current or former intimate partner. Stalking creates a paranoid type of fear.

Have you ever felt like someone was watching you? Have you ever felt paranoid that someone was following you?

For stalking victims, it's not just a feeling; it is their reality. The Stalking Prevention Awareness & Resource Center (SPARC) defines stalking as, "A pattern of behavior directed at a specific person that would cause a reasonable person to fear for the person's safety or the safety of others; or suffer substantial emotional distress." Stalking takes harassment to another level. As the definition says, you are a reasonable person. You're not exaggerating. You're not making things up. It's not paranoia. It's real. It's scary. And it can be dangerous.

You're not just frustrated, annoyed, or disgusted, but you are indeed in fear. Stalking could look like those hundreds of un-reciprocated text messages. The endless phone calls. The un-wanted advances. The unwelcomed gifts. They "randomly," yet frequently, show up where you are.

ALL NOT NORMAL!

It may have seemed like an act of endearment when they mag-ically arrived at your house uninvited. It may have even seemed innocent when they first started buying you gifts. But the price of their love escalated. Your comings and goings were mon-itored. You were tracked on apps. They showed up at your work, gym, church, and even your relative's homes. They pick locks. They check cameras (overt and covert). They memorize passwords.

This is a real concern for people in abusive relationships. Abus-ers who behave this way already control so much about you, and now no time is your own. Nowhere feels safe.

How do you leave when you're constantly "checked on?" How do you form a plan to escape when they are lurking in the shadows? How can you make a run for it when they are always waiting? Waiting at your car, the appointment, or the front door.

Most of the time, you don't leave. You don't escape. You don't make a run for it. Because if you do, your abuser may go one step further to retaliation.

-Retaliation. *It would be messier and more dangerous if I tried to leave, so I'll stay.*

This is common self-talk that victims use to convince themselves that staying is safer than the retaliation that may follow. Unfortunately, there are some terrible people in this world who will use children, family members, pets, etc., against the person trying to leave. They threaten to harm or actually harm those previously mentioned. Sometimes threats are exactly that: threats. But what if they aren't? Is it worth the risk or your kids' safety? If your dog is at stake? If your grandma has been threatened?

The National Coalition Against Domestic Violence says victims stay "based on the reality that their abuser will follow through with the threats they have used to keep them trapped: the abuser will hurt or kill them, they will hurt or kill the kids, they will win custody of the children, they will harm or kill pets or others, they will ruin their victim financially—the list goes on."

I don't know about you but threats like those hold high stakes to gamble on the abuser just bluffing. These are only a handful of the reasons people stay in abusive relationships. The cost of staying does not outweigh the cost of leaving.

3. The Fear on the other side of the relationship

A lot of people experience FOMO (fear of missing out), but I can tell you all I wanted was out. I was desperate to get out. But the reasons mentioned in Scenarios #1 and #2 kept yanking me back in fear. Every time I mustered the courage to leave, somehow, I was knocked back down. I just KNEW life had to be more than this. Relationships had to be healthier than this.

Then finally, thankfully, I left. Thank goodness, some people, like myself, have left their unhealthy relationships.

I did not have children or pets in this relationship, and I know it would have been substantially more difficult to leave if I did due to the facts of the Post-Separation Power and Control Wheel. Please review this wheel. People with children have these fears and possible realities to deal with when leaving the relationship. It is not an easy choice to leave.

For me, I thought I would be relieved when I left. I thought I would be able to relax. Instead, I was more alert and tense than before. I was consumed with fear. This is called hypervigilance. I didn't want to see him. I didn't want to run into him at the store. I didn't want to hear about what he was up to. And in a small town, I can't tell you the number of times this was a plausible occurrence. But more than anything, I was afraid I would go back.

> **"**
>
> *Relationships had to be healthier than this.*
>
> **"**

I cannot count the number of times we broke up and got back together or the times we were taking time apart or didn't want a label. Not to mention the number of instances I'd move my stuff out and eventually move it back in. I was afraid I would repeat this pattern because it was familiar and habitual.

73

I was afraid after leaving because I didn't know who I was. I had believed so many limiting stories about myself. I believed I had become this helpless, powerless, unworthy individual, and I didn't know how to find myself again. And worst of all, in order to heal the best way I knew, I had to face the pain of the past few years.

I had to stop living in defense mode and take Charlotte Joko Beck's advice, "We have to face the pain we have been running from. In fact, we need to learn to rest in it and let its searing power transform us."

A few chapters back, I mentioned there would be hard work. Now is that time. It's time to lean into the uncomfortability and pain we've been avoiding. Lean into the hard work and start healing.

Let's get to work.

Pause:

_____

_____

_____

_____

_____

Ponder:

1. In what scenarios are you living out learned helplessness? Who is playing a role in this experience?

_____

_____

_____

_____

_____

2. Which fears do you identify with from the three sections?

    1. The Fear while in the relationship

_____

_____

2. The Fear of leaving the relationship

_____

_____

3. The Fear on the other side of the relationship

_____

_____

Prayer:

Lord, I know you have not given us a Spirit of fear, but you do give us discernment when something is not right. You show us when there is something to fear and to take that fear before you. I pray for discernment to rise within my friend. I pray for the safety of my friend in these scary and dark situations. I pray Exodus 14:14, "The Lord will fight for you, you need only to be still." This "stillness" does not mean complacency or doing nothing, but it means for us to trust in and rely on You. I know you are fighting and waging war on behalf of my friend and that fear shall not win! Comfort them. Wrap them in your arms. Give them peace wherever they are reading this. Amen!

_____

_____

_____

_____

Chapter Five

Cycling Through Hope

My late Papa Joe used to say, "The test for stupidity is to repeat your errors." I thought about all the times I went back to him and tried to count how many times I let him come back to me. I think Papa Joe would consider those encounters errors or perhaps a lapse in judgment. Would he also consider that stupidity? Would he consider me stupid?

Gosh, I sure hope not. That seems so harsh.

Papa, you're only seeing part of the story. I promise.

I wrestle with that word. Stupid. My stupidity. It's not very uplifting, nor a word I want to associate myself with. I know what Papa Joe meant. He meant to stop and process a situation; to examine what was going on in my life. He also meant I should assess whether this relationship is good, if this job is working out, or if this friendship is mutually beneficial.

Papa Joe impressed me that I needed to evaluate things with a fine-toothed comb, such as going back to my partner, staying at the job, and reconciling with the parent instead of cutting them off or remaining on the team.

But when you are drowning in a toxic relationship, irrational thought can be so strong that it defies common sense. No one on the outside looking in can fathom why we return and most of the time, we can't articulate how we came to this decision either.

The reasoning is complicated. It's messy and mixed with heaps of emotions and memories.

I'm not stupid.

We aren't stupid.

We need to release that lie and let go of that undermining description of ourselves. Those "errors" were hazed with hope. Hope for a better tomorrow or a hope to go back to when things were good.

It was hope. Not stupidity.

You were hoping, weren't you?

It is a hope that a certain someone will change, that they will learn from their mistakes, or that they will appreciate who they have in front of them. When my hope would decline, somehow, it always found its second wind like a recharge. Somewhere in my reserves, a surplus of energy, motivation, and determination would emerge.

When I played sports, this second wind was a good thing. It

was a life line to finish the practice or game strong. Give it all I had so I could be proud of myself when the buzzer sounded or the whistle was blown. Similarly, I mustered enough hope to believe in him again. I dug deep to try one more time.

But every time I said, "Just one more time," it turned into another time. And another time after that. And another time after that. This recharge was not life-giving.

The hope was cyclical, and it was destructive.

I just KNEW he had greatness inside of him, and I even saw shimmering glimpses of the man I knew he could be. These moments were like golden nuggets. You don't give away, trade-in, or throw away golden nuggets. You protect and cherish them.

Maybe your shimmering glimpses look like one of these.

— Your friend finally initiated the conversation AND asked how YOU were.

— Your boss is on a good mood streak. What a change of pace!

— Your mom said something nice. Was that a compliment? Directed towards me?

— Your coach actually acknowledged your contribution. Finally! I've been working so hard!

— Your spouse didn't complain about the food and even thanked you for making dinner.

They are little pieces of good. Most of the time, they shock us because these glimpses of good are so rare. They are gifts we treasure because we don't know when the next one will arise.

We pray they will last. We pray the change will stick because this is what we've been waiting for! This is proof of progress!

A hope for a better tomorrow.

Right?

Or maybe this is, "Just one more time."

We cling to that hope so tightly that reality runs for cover under the glaze of the glimpses. The sad reality is that usually, these glimpses are just that: glimpses. Short moments in time. They are temporary. They are fleeting. They don't stay. They most generally do not change. They, more often than not, revert to their original state.

-Your friend again expects you to start the conversation and listen to them the whole time.

-Your boss's moodiness rears its ugly head. You never know what you're walking into.

-Your mom's passive aggressive (or straight aggressive) remarks resurface.

-Your coach goes back to criticizing you, complaining about you, or completely ignoring you.

-Your spouse's gratitude reverts to demands and unrealistic expectations.

This, my friends, is what I call cyclical hope.

Cyclical hope will leave you disappointed and aching for the good to return.

> **We cling to that hope so tightly that reality runs for cover under the glaze of the glimpses.**

I often use the phrase, "Well, that escalated quickly," as a joke when something gets out of hand too fast, or the mood changes from fun and lighthearted to somber and sober instantly. I say it to crack a joke into the tension and to allow everyone to take a step back and evaluate how the conversation turned.

When clinging to hope in an unhealthy relationship, it always seems like we go from good to bad in an instant. As quickly as the good appears, it vanishes. Our delight dims, and reality marches back in. The bad comes rushing in, destroying everything in its wake, and I think, "Well, that escalated quickly."

But what I've learned is that it didn't escalate quickly at all. The relationship escalated cyclically. We cycle through hope that they can change and are changed for good.

They really are committed to seeing the therapist. They actually do see our efforts. Deep down, they appreciate our contribution. They finally meant the apology.

Then the cycle starts again. The behavior is temporary because the change never reaches its core. It lingered over the surface to give us enough optimism to believe in them once more. The best apology is lasting, core-changing behavior that reaches the depths of their innermost being. Unfortunately, in unhealthy relationships, they continue to cycle through a vicious set of patterns to lure us back in every time.

Remember when I mentioned the statistic that it usually takes seven times for a victim to leave for good?

> **Don't ignore the tension. Don't discount what you're feeling.**

You might not be in a domestic violent relationship. You might not consider yourself a victim. This person might not have abused you in the way culture typically defines abuse.

But, then again, maybe this is you. Maybe you've been reading these chapters and you're realizing this is your reality.

Domestic violence does not discriminate against age, religion, gender, income, race, etc. Sadly, all are fair game to falling prey to narcissistic abusers. No matter what, you know your situation better than anyone else. I cannot define for you what your relationship is like. But it's probably a safe bet if you've made it this far in the book something resonates with you.

Don't ignore the tension. Don't discount what you're feeling.

Maybe it's for you, your friend, or a family member. This statistic speaks directly to domestic violent relationships, but what if that speaks to *all* unhealthy relationships? I think it does.

However you define your relationship, that cyclical hope keeps luring you back.

There are many types of abuse, and we've thought about leaving at least hundreds of times. So, why didn't we act on it? Or if we did, why did we go back? Five times. Seven times. Ten times.

I said it before, and I'll repeat it. I wish I wasn't a contributor to that statistic, but I am.

And if I'm being completely honest, the back and forth of the breakup and makeup was exhilarating.

I *had* to make a big deal to get his attention, to let him know I was serious. I *had* to storm out to make him realize what he was missing. I *had* to yell. We *had* to fight.

The blow-up *had* to happen. Then, I *had* to apologize (every time).

Little did I know, he needed me to blow up. It benefited him if I engaged in the argument, if I fought back, if I yelled, or if I stormed out. He was relying on "reactive abuse." Breakthesilencedv.org says, "Abusers rely on 'reactive abuse' because it is their 'proof' that the victim is unstable and mentally ill. The abuser will hold these reactions against the victims indefinitely."

Essentially, every time I retaliated, it was used as evidence that I was abusing him and not the other way around. It was used as ammunition in our next argument and always left me feeling crazy. But I justified thinking that if this was the only way to get him to notice me, at least I felt I was seen.

It all came back to that small four-lettered word that promises it will all be better.

"Hope."

So tiny. So powerful.

They will change. They will never do it again. They will never say that again. They will never treat you that way again. We can get back to where we used to be. Who we used to be.

"Hope."

A small four-lettered word whose promise diminishes as quickly as you return to the relationship.

Whether you consider your relationship to be an ongoing frustration with a manipulative coworker or a detrimental entanglement with an abusive family member, the patterns can be witnessed in any unhealthy relationship. Eventually, you will be exhausted from the one-sided investment. The starvation and desperation you feel for attention, acceptance, and love will create a dysfunctional tsunami. You'll keep longing, striving, and receiving a rejection that leaves you feeling inadequate and exposed.

Knowing what to look for and understanding the patterns of toxicity can empower you to implement boundaries so that cycling through hope will cease to crush your spirits.

American psychologist Lenore Edna Walker, who founded the Domestic Violence Institute, discovered there are phases you can use to describe this cyclical nature. She refers to the cycle in four phases: Tensions Building, Incident, Reconciliation, and Calm. If you research it further, you might find synonyms for the phases, like "Explosion" for "Incident" or "Honeymoon" for "Calm," but essentially, they mean the same thing. I want to deconstruct these phases with you and give language to what you have been or someone you love has been experiencing.

Tensions Building Phase

The abused person feels growing tension and stress. It's heavy, and it sits in the middle of every conversation and encounter. And yet, no one addresses it. No one speaks to the tension. No one questions the stress.

A part of the tension stems from fear. We are afraid to speak to the tension because we don't want an explosion. We don't want to say or do the wrong thing. We desperately try to cling to the peace and harmony that we see slipping away.

We ask ourselves, "What is the least amount of information I can give to pacify but not enough to make me more vulnerable?"

I could always feel the tension brewing. I never knew when the eruption would be, but I knew in my bones that it was coming. It was the calm before the storm, the quiet moment before the tornado started to swirl.

The silence stems from confusion. We don't understand why their actions display a vast disconnect from reality. We don't understand why their reactions are widely disproportionate to the situation. We don't understand why it's the end of the world to talk calmly or talk at all about what's going on that caused them to become upset.

Yet, I distinctly remember being told I was the dramatic one (insert sass and eye-rolling). Hmm. That sure is confusing.

The other part originates from denial. This can't be happening again. After all, they promised. They eloquently laid out a step-by-step process on how they would ensure this would never happen again.

I have it in writing! (pulls out phone and scrolls several times to the top of the lengthiest text in the history of ever)

They promised and pledged. They guaranteed and professed, and here we are, again. We try to control the situation and avoid the person's anger. These are our "walking on eggshells" moments, which have successfully created tension. From here, we are set up to experience the much anticipated and equally dreaded Incident Phase.

Incident Phase

In my opinion, the Incident Phase is the worst and possibly the scariest phase. There is an explosion of emotion that results in one or many abusive behaviors. Initially, this is the shortest stage, but it increases in length and severity over time. It could be present in the form of verbal, financial, emotional, sexual, or physical abuse. It could look like anger, blaming, arguing, threats, intimidation, etc.

More specifically, it could look like being cut off from the bank account, threatening to hurt you, the kids, or pets, arguing over trivial matters, destroying your personal belongings, and leaving you for days. Or maybe it presents itself in the workplace by lashing out in the meeting room or slamming office doors. Maybe your abuser decides to go the route of making a scene in public, humiliating you in front of friends, family members, or coworkers.

The examples go on, and the list never stops. The creativity of the incident is equally vicious as it is endless. And every time we revisit this phase, the incidents gain momentum. They escalate with tenacity and build with terror. It is not uncommon that the next incident is worse than the last.

So, why do we return?

Reconciliation Phase

They apologize. They make promises that they will change or they will never do it again. They might even cry, and those tears seem incredibly sincere and true. Or, on the opposite end, they might give excuses, and often they will blame you. They may deny the event occurred or say the event wasn't as bad as you claim it to be (See Chapter 3: Massively Manipulated).

Overall, this phase resembles courting. You could ask for almost anything you want at this stage, and you'll get it. Unfortunately, it could be used against you later, saying you're ungrateful and entitled, but at that moment you think they are giving you the world.

If it's a romantic relationship, they may start to take you on dates again. They might buy you flowers or cook dinner. They might even surprise you with gifts, schmoozing and romancing to erase the terror.

If it's a professional relationship, they might give you the afternoon off or an extra day paid vacation. (Don't worry; coffee is on them today. Surprise lunch for the office this week!) They might build you up with words, encouraging you to go for that promotion or congratulating you on your latest project. They buy and give, praying you'll forget the Human Resources Department exists.

If it's a familial relationship, they don't say anything insensitive. They don't push your buttons. They applaud you for being a great mom. They encourage you to hold firm to your boundaries. They are in awe of your wisdom and forward-thinking. They are so proud of you and how much further along you are than when they were at your age.

They will say whatever and do whatever to regain control. Yet you don't realize it as them regaining both power and control. You perceive it as them making amends. They are trying to get back into your good graces. They are genuinely making an effort. They are trying. They are doing the best they can. (Can you feel that cyclical hope creeping back in?)

We begin to think, *"Maybe I overreacted. Maybe I took things a little too far. Maybe I didn't see the situation clearly. They were going through a rough time. I need to extend grace. After all, this is how I would want to be treated if the situation was reversed."*

Do you see it? Do you see how tricky and sneaky this phase is? I've almost convinced myself to go back to these imagined scenarios. I want to see and believe that people are inherently good inside. I want to extend grace because that is what I have been taught. I want to forgive, and I long to forget.

And then it returns. The cyclical hope.

From the Reconciliation Phase to the Calm or "honeymoon" Stage, there is love, cyclical hope, and fear.

Calm Phase

Time passes. The initial feelings of disgust, rage, hurt, and survival have lessened. You slowly resurface. Timid. Compliant. Exhausted. We savor the morsels of hope sprinkled our way. The incident is further removed from our memory. Was it really as bad as we thought it was?

They haven't yelled. They haven't said anything cruel, sarcastic, or demeaning. They haven't broken anything. They haven't slammed anything. They haven't taken anything away. Essentially, no abuse is taking place. Maybe that was the last time.

Is this what peace feels like? Is this here to stay?

Hope is rising. This is what we wanted, what we longed for. This is the person we just knew they could be.

This, my friends, is traumatic bonding. A medically reviewed Heathline article written by Crystal Raypole says, "This emotional attachment, known as a trauma bond, develops out of a repeated cycle of abuse, devaluation, and positive reinforcement." Each time the victim experiences the cycle of abuse, their bond becomes tighter with their abuser.

During the calm phase, when the apologies, gifts, and affection are flowing, so are the victim's hormones. Raypole continues by saying there is a sense of relief due to dopamine coursing through the victim's veins and any intimacy received releases oxytocin. Both of these hormones add to the strengthening of the traumatic bond. The stronger the bond, the harder it is to break away.

It's hard to say how long the calm phase will last. Sometimes, it depends on how explosive the incident was and how long the reconciliation took.

" The stronger the bond, the harder it is to break away. "

But after some time, it always returns.

Slowly, it creeps back in. Do you sense it?

Hello, tension. I cannot say it's good to feel you again.

89

And the cycle begins again.

So, if the cycle stays the same, how do we get off this ride? I want to suggest three concepts to help you in the cycle of hope. These three concepts have helped me tremendously on my journey. In different scenarios and different relationships I have to remind myself of these concepts.

Avoid the Savior Complex

Almost daily, I would rehearse, "How can I avoid making them upset today? What should I do to make them happy today? When should I talk to them about ____."

Same situation, different day. I'm sure you have your list of *How Can I's*, *What Should I's*, and *When Do I's*. You're frequently thinking about that other person and constantly putting their needs and desires above your own. It's in our nature to help, assist, and be present. But we enter dangerous territory when we begin to believe that we are the ones who are there to save them from themselves.

In her online *Huffington Post* article, Dr. Carol Morgan describes this territory as the savior complex, also known as the messiah complex (Morgan, 2017, para 7). In an unhealthy relationship we begin to believe we need to be the ones to motivate, assist, and change them. They cannot do it on their own, and they need us.

In turn, we begin to invest even more time, energy, and resources into helping them. We won't admit they have become a project for us, but we are deeply invested in seeing them grow, mature, and fight off whatever demons they are facing.

We want to know why they are like this. We want to get to the root of the problem. We want to help, but at what cost? And when the cycle makes its rounds and the incident inevitably occurs, we feel responsible for their actions because somehow we didn't do enough. We didn't say the right things. We didn't try hard enough.

The savior complex is dangerous because we aren't called to be people's saviors. Jesus remains the only person who saves others from themselves and their sins. My assignment is not to save people from themselves. Each person holds a personal responsibility for their well-being and their actions. Whether they accept that responsibility or not is out of my control; I cannot force someone to be responsible. I cannot save them from themselves.

You cannot help someone who doesn't want help. You may never be able to logically understand why they are the way they are or why they did what they did. You might not ever be able to close that looping question the way you want to. Instead of focusing on figuring them out and fixing them, focus on you.

Leave the saving up to Jesus. I promise it's much more freeing that way.

Re-examine Incidents as a Cycle, not Isolated Occurrences

I struggled with this concept because I was unaware of the cycle. I didn't understand that abuse disguises itself in the forms of put-downs, boundary-pushing, intimidation, and manipulation. I didn't even realize I was being manipulated!

> *Abuse disguises itself in the forms of put-downs, boundary-pushing, intimidation, and manipulation.*

And if you're in a relationship with a narcissist, these are just a few of their many strategies to control you. Eleanor Payson says, "The behaviors that accomplish this outcome have a variety of forms but generally fall into one of the following nine types: Admiration/Idealization; Martyr/Guilt; Intimidation; Distraction; Devaluing; Repetitive Criticism; Double Message/Double Bind; Projection; and Emotional Hostage." For an in-depth view of these nine types, check out *The Wizard of Oz and Other Narcissists* again. Payson not only describes each type, but she also provides insight on how to protect yourself and set boundaries.

I didn't realize there was a set of phases and patterns we were cycling through. I treated every incident as an isolated occurrence instead of recognizing them as a string of examples leading back to the abuse.

If I lost my car keys, I was careless. If I didn't give him a ride, I was selfish. If my shoes were left out, I was messy. If I lost my balance, I was clumsy.

Each of these little things was irritation and annoyance. To some people, these might sound like petty, unimportant observations, but these were examples of early warning signs of my unhealthy relationship. They appear to be insignificant and unrelated incidents, but they were consistent and used to demean, belittle, label, and control. They were warning signs begging for my attention.

The incidents I experienced progressed. I was the butt of jokes the muse for his comedy. Secrets swirled in deleted text messages and private phone calls.

Early in the relationship, I treated each remark as an isolated occurrence. It was one moment in time. It wasn't worth mentioning this time. But the comments never went away. They persisted and perpetuated. Was it necessary to address the remark this time? The degrading statements were compounding, and the detriment to my character was evident.

I was afraid to confront the issue because he would undermine, twist, blame, and retaliate. I was left apologizing, retreating, and mending. This should have been evidence that something was really wrong. It should have confirmed that this relationship was unhealthy. Yet, I had been trained to take the accusations, the outbursts, and the blame.

When he punched the wall, he was just upset. When he destroyed the door, it wasn't his fault. When he locked me in the bathroom, he just wanted to talk. When he stole my purse, he just wanted my attention.

Seeing these actions listed on paper is sobering. It's evident to see how the cycle works because, in life, the abuser's infractions aren't listed one after another. In between each of these memories are moments of reconciliation and calm. Treating them as isolated occurrences was easier to dismiss but not any less damaging. When I began to recognize them as a cycle, I began to see the bigger picture. I saw the string of events all interwoven. They were entangled with my cyclical hope that he would change and the ideal, romanticized relationship I grappled to maintain.

The remarks, the angry outbursts, and the control all led back to abuse. There was no more denying the obvious. I couldn't look past the hurt (physically, emotionally, and psychologically) plaguing my heart.

It seems innocent to question why they acted out or said what they did. We can go around and around trying to figure out what exactly happened and why. We search for the root reason to make sense of their actions. Maybe the reason is tied to their past, or maybe it's connected to their current season of life. Maybe it was a lapse in judgment.

We are looking for a connection to comprehend the occurrence. But the only connection you'll find is a compilation of unhealthy incidents cycling their course. I know you were trying to help the situation by helping them; however they still see each occurrence as a one-time event. They don't perceive a problem and certainly don't believe they have any responsibility in the matter.

So, if we can't save them from themselves (Remember, leave the saving to Jesus) and we recognize the occurrences as a cycle, what do we do?

Transfer Cyclical Hope Into Ultimate Hope

Being a Christian I struggled immensely with the thought that I was giving up if I walked away. If I let go of this relationship, I would not be Christ-like. I knew Christ loved this person, so I needed my love to mirror Christ's.

What I didn't understand is that you can love someone and still leave. Sometimes, the most loving thing to do for you and them is to leave. You aren't called to absorb the shocks of their wrath.

Again, each situation is unique. Maybe leaving looks different for you. It might look like leaving a certain set of expectations. It might be separating yourself from particular situations. It might look like relocating or reallocating your time, energy, and resources. Maybe it's reestablishing boundaries. In my situation, leaving the actual relationship was what became necessary.

I hung up on several Bible verses that I felt bound me to him. The first one was 1 Corinthians 13:13, "Three things will last forever- faith, hope, and love- and the greatest of these is love" (New Living Translation). I wanted my love to conquer his anger. I wanted it to be bigger than our fights and stronger than his sarcastic demeanor. My faith was intact, and my hope was firm. Above all else, I needed my love to overcome all the bad.

My love did not have that power. And Christ's love does not hurt.

Christ's love does not sound like fighting, bickering, and lashing out. Christ's love does not feel like the stinging wounds of physical or emotional abuse. Christ's love does not command me to give up my safety or peace for someone else.

Another verse that perplexed me was Matthew 5:39, "But I tell you, do not resist an evil person. If anyone slaps you on the right cheek, turn to them the other cheek also" (New International Version).

I read that and assumed that I had to ignore his blatant attacks on my self-esteem. I thought it gave him license to say or do whatever, and I just had to take it. Turning the other cheek isn't a free pass for people to treat you like garbage. Christ created us in His image (Gen 1:27), and I know He isn't garbage. Therefore, He legitimately cannot reproduce garbage. So, we shouldn't let others treat us in that manner.

I came to realize that I kept placing my hope in this relationship. I kept placing my hope in him to change. I would search for confirmation of his change when I should have been seeking my hope in Christ. My hope was misplaced. I don't think it's wrong to be hopeful for someone. We want to see people succeed, advance, and grow, but not at the cost of our self-esteem and safety.

Lamentations 3:21-23 says, "Yet this I call to mind and therefore I have hope: Because of the Lord's great love we are not consumed, for his compassions never fail. They are new every morning; great is your faithfulness" (New International Version).

The Lord's love was going to see me through this transition from cyclical hope to ultimate

> **The Lord's love was going to see me through this transition from cyclical hope to ultimate hope.**

hope. I would no longer be consumed with false hope. The Lord wouldn't fail me because He is good and faithful. I knew I had to release the cyclical hope because it was no longer serving me. Rather, it was undermining what the Lord wanted to do through me, and ultimately, it was enabling and reinforcing unhealthy behaviors every time I returned.

Lastly, I repeatedly ruminated over Isaiah 40:31, "But those who hope in the Lord will renew their strength. They will soar on wings like eagles; they will run and not grow weary, they will walk and not be faint" (New International Version). I needed strength to transfer my hope solely to the Lord because I had become so accustomed to placing it in man. I needed a reminder that placing my hope in the Lord was far more effective and yielded a much higher return than placing it in a person.

When I released cyclical hope, I released my misplaced responsibility to save him which is to change him. The Lord would do the saving and the changing, and ironically, a lot of change was headed my way. I didn't realize how timely and encouraging Isaiah 40:31 would become in the next stage of my healing journey.

Pause:

_____

_____

_____

_____

_____

Ponder:

1. Where and how do you see cyclical hope showing up in your unhealthy relationships?

_____

_____

_____

_____

_____

2. Which of the three concepts for change do you resonate with the most? Why?

_____

_____

_____

_____

_____

Prayer:

Lord, I pray my friend doesn't have to go through one more cycle. I pray cyclical hope stops today and that their hope is ultimately placed in you! I pray they will not be swayed by the reconciliation phase. I pray Psalm 119:105 over their life. That Your Word would be a lamp to their feet and a light for their path—that You would begin to speak directly and clearly to them about what to do next in their situation. Amen.

_____

_____

_____

_____

_____

Chapter Six

Breaking the Ties

As I began writing this chapter, my soon-to-be two-year old sat beside me on the couch. Her legs entangled in the blanket that she demanded I wrap her in. But now, she was clearly over this cuddly moment and wanted to get out of it.

She squirmed and thrashed. She kicked and cried.

"I sukkkk Mommy!"

"Are you 'stuck'?"

"Yeah! I STUCK!" (this time, emphasis on the "T")

She wasn't really stuck because I was there. But she squirmed at a frantic pace that she couldn't figure out how to untangle herself from the engulfing blanket. The blanket was too large and heavy for her to maneuver by herself. She needed my help initially, but she had to do it herself in her independent two-year old fashion. If she had slowed down and stayed still long enough for me to assist her, she wouldn't have had this panicked moment.

Aren't we the same?

I mean, I hope you know how to get out of a blanket (well maybe not the chunky knitted ones that threaten to take your toes with them). But we are the same, just like my daughter.

We do the same thing with our healing. We move frantically to get as far away from the hurt and turmoil that we don't slow down long enough to know what still has us snared. We aren't sure of what we've broken off from our lives and what is still broken within us.

We don't want to slow down. We internally chant…

Keep going. Ignore it. Push it down. It'll go away.

Oh no, I'm feeling some unwanted, uncomfortable emotions! MOVE FASTER!

So, we keep twisting and turning in that blanket, trying to break out without ever truly experiencing freedom. We waste so much energy trying to do it ourselves when the Ultimate Healer is just waiting for His invitation.

In the past, I didn't want to invite the Lord into my healing. I didn't want Him to see the mess I had created. I knew I wasn't perfect in my relationships, and I was the one who got myself into the messes. So, I felt responsible for getting myself out of them and heal from the alone. But every time I took charge, I didn't heal.

I ended up:

— Harboring resentment

— Rehearsing the injustice

— Distrusting people

— Lashing out

— Hiding my insecurities

— Burying the pain

When I didn't heal, I decayed.

Just like my daughter relied on me to help her get "unstuck," I needed the Lord's help to navigate this healing journey. In Christian circles, people talk about breaking ties. Most generally, they are referring to soul ties, but I want to cover a couple more with you. In relationships, there are people, places, and things that keep us connected to them. Ties that remind us of them or draw us back in.

In order to begin the healing process, one great place to start is breaking ties. Some happen naturally, while others we must be intentional to sever. This is an assess and reassess chapter. You'll want to refer back to this throughout your healing journey and see where you're at with breaking the ties.

The ties we will touch on in this chapter are financial, relational, physical, spiritual, emotional, and sexual. I will briefly cover each of these areas. It's not an exhaustive list or extensive coverage, as some of these ties could be entire books themselves. These are not in any particular order, and you might not be able to do all of them depending on your situation. You might break several ties all at once or in a single day, or it might take some sifting through and processing. Some, unfortunately, might require legality.

Remember, these ties will be based on the relationship you have in question. Not all may apply to you, or maybe, while you're reading, it brings another tie you need to lose to your memory. For those of you who are list people, especially check-list people, this will be your jam!

Financial- What has both your names on it? This could be checking accounts, saving accounts, or investment accounts. Credit cards. Bills. Whose name is on the electric, water, phone, and trash bill? This gets tricky. Whose name is on the lease? The mortgage? The car loan? Any loan?

What have you purchased together? Thankfully, when I left, we had a somewhat healthy conversation about who kept the couch, who got the dresser, and where the bed was going.

But some of you didn't have that luxury. Some of you left in the middle of the night or early in the morning, and you left it all behind. It was a huge sacrifice for safety, but thankfully those ties were completely broken.

What about sentimental items? I am not suggesting gathering that box of letters and pictures and hosting a private or semi-private burn party. As tempting as that might be, I'm not confident it will give you the healing and closure you are hopefully looking for. But in all seriousness, were there any gifts that you didn't want to tie to them? When you put that watch on, stare at that ring, or use that mug, will it be too much for your heart to handle?

What if they are the ones writing your paycheck? Been there and lived that. You've exhausted your options of frank conversations and boundary setting. You've sought out upper-management assistance and even support from HR, but they've all let you down. The promises fell flat and were not followed through.

Sometimes, switching departments might be a healthy option for you, or a completely new company could be the answer to breaking that tie. It might be time to polish that resume and do some networking.

Relational- When their friends are your friends. Awesome. Unfortunately, there might be some friendship breakups within the tie breakings. People usually pick sides, or if it gets too messy, they slowly back away from the connection. You may make the decision that they can stay acquaintances, but to protect yourself from further hurt, they don't get access to you or your heart like they used to.

Which brings me to family members. Ugh, this one is so difficult for me. A big lie I believed was that I could not take healthy action or set appropriate boundaries because they were my family members. I see them regularly, and it is just "easier" to put up with them than to have the hard conversations or make the changes.

CALLING ALL HERO PEOPLE PLEASING ADULT CHILDREN. Yes, there are many of us out there. I have something important to tell you.

"No" is a complete sentence.

I'm just going to throw this out there. See where it lands. Maybe you'll pick it up.

> When you keep telling everyone else, "Yes," you are, in turn, repeatedly telling yourself, "No."

66

You aren't giving up on them. You are finally showing up for yourself.

99

Saying no isn't harsh. It isn't cruel. It isn't mean. You can't do everything always, and even if you could, don't!

You aren't giving up on them. You are finally showing up for yourself.

Let's say that out loud and make it personal.

I'm not giving up on them. I'm finally showing up for myself.

Here is a tricky and messy aspect of relational ties. Some of you might have children with the person you need to break ties with. Obviously, you can't not see this person. If you're co-parenting or sharing custody, there will be interaction. There will be some form of communication. But you can still have boundaries. You can still show up for yourself and your children and break as much of that tie as possible.

I strongly recommend Lysa Terkeurst's book *Good Boundaries and Goodbyes* as well as Dr. Henry Cloud's and Dr. John Townsend's book *Boundaries*. I pray those two resources give you more clarity and tools in order to navigate life when precious children are involved.

Lastly, let's address social media. Do a purge because it is necessary. There's no reason to see their feed. You keep checking their status, reels, and stories to ensure they are miserable. But really, the only one miserable is you! And no, you don't need to be friends with their grandma, aunt, cousin, etc., so that you can keep tabs on them. Release it!

Physical- This section is not about being physically intimate. Read further down for that. This is about location, location, location. Where did you hang out? Did you frequent certain restaurants, parks, bars, etc.?

I remember the first time I walked into a Longhorn Steakhouse after my separation. I sobbed into my bowl of lobster mac n cheese (I wish they still had this on their menu). I didn't even get to enjoy my meal, and I'm pretty sure I scarred the waitress for life.

I thought, "Great, now Longhorn Steakhouse is ruined for me."

But it wasn't a forever thing. My first encounter at the restaurant was too much for me to handle. Memories surfaced too fast for me to process and deal with. I needed time and space from physical reminders of my relationship. I needed the break.

And no, I didn't frequent where I knew he would be or places we used to go to together where he might be. There was a moment when I felt defiant, like, "Heck no, he needs to be the one to stay away!"

It's like a game of chicken. Who can outlast the other in the most uncomfortable, unhealthy way. How many eye rolls and death glares can we beam to their brain while simultaneously dodging their radiating heat of hate? How awkward can we make this situation until one of us has had enough and leaves?

Thankfully, I recognized that defiance was ugly of me. I wasn't giving in by staying away. I had a choice, and now, so do you. You can choose to intentionally place yourself in locations that will make you miserable, or you can work on your healing.

Some people call that losing, but I call it choosing me. And I chose healing.

Spiritual- This tie-breaking makes me so sad. Sometimes, it's a pastor who has hurt you deeply or a church member who has wounded you. Maybe it's someone you dated in the church. Whatever the case, the breaking of this tie isn't fair.

"

Some people call that losing, but I call it choosing me. And I chose healing.

"

More than likely, they'll be adamant about staying and that you should forgive and forget. They'd remind you of the church slogan, "What would Jesus Do?" (WWJD).

Hot garbage.

Jesus wouldn't have mistreated you in the first place. Jesus wouldn't have wounded you, scared you, abused you, or cheated on you. Also, Jesus is the only one who can forgive AND forget.

I recognize that the church is not perfect, nor is its people, and we are all sinners. We can talk about forgiveness later, but right now, we are talking about healthy boundaries for you. You might have to stop going to that group for a while, or you might want a complete break and find another church for a fresh start.

In her book *The Lord is My Courage*, K. J. Ramsey states, "Building the kingdom of God is no excuse for bullying." Spiritual abuse is sickening, and it is happening more than we know or would like to admit. Excessively working people and shaming them in the name of ministry is disgusting, and I cannot recommend Ramsey's book enough.

Emotional- ALL THE CLAPS FOR THERAPY! People who go to counseling are brave and healthier than those who keep talking about counseling but wallow in their self-pity and dysfunction. I support therapy all the way. I'm actually researching therapists in my area in this season of my life right now.

Research them. Find one you resonate with. Try it out. Don't jive with that therapist? Try again! I say once more, "YAY THERAPY!"

Also, quit watching the sappy movies that make you hate your current life. I'm all for a good crying movie sesh with a slice (or two) from Cake Bar, but not on repeat. I'd rather work on my overall health than wallow in pity and cake crumbles.

And for the love of everything, quit listening to the sad and mad breakup songs. You know what I'm talking about. One minute, they are bawling because the relationship is over, and the next they are raining fire on their ex.

Stop listening to it. Take a break. Switch the station. Hit next.

Instead of watching or listening to things that are stirring up all these emotions and memories foryou, another way to help break the ties is to practice journaling. It's like a diary but for our century. You get everything out on paper. Very cathartic. Sometimes therapeutic. And since you're finding a therapist, you can also ask them what they suggest.

Sexual- Soul ties can for sure be its own book, and I am not a soul tie expert. But this is what I do know from my own experience.

One evening, I took a hot shower. It wasn't going to be one of those short rinse-off showers. This was a decompress-contemplate-all-my-life-decisions shower. I hadn't been in the shower long before grief overwhelmed me. I collapsed to my knees clenching my chest.

How could I feel this much pain and still be alive? I cried until there weren't any more tears to give. I braced my hands on the bathroom floor as I tried to suck in a full breath of air. This was panic.

Is this what dying feels like? I saw no end to the misery and pain enveloping me.

I didn't understand. I lived in a different house. I started counseling. I had broken all the ties. So, why did I want him to hug me in this dilemma of exhausting grief? I couldn't figure out why, after everything I had been through... everything he had put me through, I still wanted to be close to him. To be intimate with him.

The answer is soul ties.

What is important to understand about soul ties is that they aren't bad! The tie itself isn't bad. What is important is who you connect that tie to. And what's also wild is that soul ties don't just have to be sexual as it can happen in friendships and families. It can happen at work. It can happen in ministry. It can happen with anyone whom you have a deep connection with.

Moralrevolution.com describes a soul tie as "a tridimensional experience: spirit, soul, and body." In regards to sexual soul ties, when you have sex with someone, it creates a bond between you and that person. It is so much more than just a physical act. You are giving a part of yourself to them and vice versa. You are giving them influence over you.

This bond happens both in men and women. Dr. Daniel Amen explained in his book *Change Your Brain, Change Your Life* that "Whenever a person is sexually involved with another person, neurochemical changes occur in both their brains that encourage limbic bonding. Limbic bonding is the reason casual sex doesn't really work for most people on a whole mind and body level." It's a bond whether they are seeking it or not, and usually, women form the attachment quicker and deeper because the woman's limbic system is larger than the man's. When breaking the sexual soul tie, it is difficult for men but actually more difficult for women.

Going further, the speakers at Moral Revolution say, "Sex is like gluing two pieces of wood together and the next day ripping them apart." My pieces of wood weren't being ripped apart a day later but rather years later. This would explain the agonizing torment I felt. This tie had to be broken.

Tom Crandall and Cole Zick do a beautiful job of describing soul ties, their pure intention, and how to break them when they are unhealthy. Here's your homework– check out their podcast video on soul ties. It's on Moral Revolution's blog and worth the 24-minute watch.

…

All of these ties, financial, relational, physical, spiritual, emotional, and sexual, must be assessed in your life. Excuses enable, and avoidance never works.

When we don't break these ties, it reminds me of a silly, innocent game I play with my daughter. We are both playing on the ground, and she tries to crawl away. Right before she gets away, I grab one of her feet and pull her back to me. We repeat this over and over again. She tries to crawl away. I pull her back. She will even stick one of her feet back towards me to make it easier for me to pull her back.

Those ties will never let you fully go. You'll try to crawl away, but then you'll be pulled back. Don't make it easier for you to be pulled back! Put in the work and break those ties.

Do you know what breaking these ties gives you? Freedom.

When you experience that freedom, it begins your journey of healing. Breaking the ties is the first step towards restoration. God can, and He does restore when we submit the broken pieces of our lives to Him. He can restore and heal us to a beauty far more than we can hope or imagine.

Pause:

_____

_____

_____

_____

_____

Ponder:

1. Which tie(s) do you still need to break?

_____

_____

_____

_____

2. What is your plan to break those ties?

_____

_____

_____

_____

_____

Prayer:

Lord, I pray for revelation on what ties still need to be broken in my friend's life. I pray their heart is receptive to receive your counsel and trust your plan. I speak against the lie that they are losing, giving up, or giving in. I pray they believe Psalm 107:14 which says "[You] led them from the darkness and deepest gloom; [You] snapped their chains" (New Living Translation). I pray they begin to see with fresh eyes that they are choosing to heal and you are snapping chains. That they are choosing to show up for themselves. I pray they continually return to you to assess these ties and take another step towards healing. Amen.

_____

_____

_____

_____

_____

Chapter Seven

A Mixed Bag of Healing

Have you ever received a gift bag, without knowing its content? You see the tissue paper, but you have no clue if you're going to like the contents within the bag. It's a risky gamble, but the giver is anxiously looking at you, waiting for you to open the surprise.

That's how I think most of us feel in regard to healing. We have received a bag but don't know what's inside. Whether physical, mental, emotional, or spiritual, most of us believe in healing in some facet of our lives. Or we have believed in healing in the past.

We believe we've each been given a bag, but we don't know what the contents will be. Will I pull back the tissue paper and be overwhelmed by complete miraculous healing? Will I tear into partial healing with an ache that lingers for life? Or do I get the mixed bag of healing where the diagnosis leaves and suddenly it returns? Then it leaves, and then it returns, giving me the gruesome gift of whiplash and worry.

Maybe, I tear expectantly into an EMPTY bag. Greeted with the crushing defeat of no healing at all.

Can we switch bags with someone else? Can we trade ours in? Can I pretend this isn't my bag?

I don't want to receive this bag. I want to give it back. I personally received a bag I wouldn't wish on anyone.

For me, I realized I was free but incredibly broken. In need of healing in more than one way.

I walked into the doctor's office, checked in, and sat down. I believed every nurse, doctor, and patient knew why I was there. They could sense my shame. I reeked of guilt. Shoulders slumped, I avoided eye contact. I wrapped my jacket tight around my sides, hoping I would feel secure.

Negative. Nothing was certain except my lapse in judgment so many lapses.

I felt so dirty. So degraded. So cheap.

I heard the whisper to my soul, *"I love you."*

"Oh no! God knows I'm here too!" Insert compounding anxiety and anguish.

I darted for the bathroom to let the tears flow freely. I repeatedly smacked my hands into my head.

"Stupid, stupid, stupid," I repeated. My stomach was in knots, and I felt the nausea rising.

I knew I had to see my doctor, but I didn't connect the fact that my omnipresent God would follow me to the appointment. I didn't realize He would accompany me into the blood lab.

How could God love me in this moment?

I heard the nurse summoning my name. I retreated from the bathroom and followed the nurse.

Height. Weight. Vitals.

"Why are you here today?"

How many times am I going to have to answer this question today? My answer ended our small talk real quick.

"The doctor will be in to see you shortly."

"Thank you," I said with my head hung low in defeat.

My doctor walked in a few minutes later, and we circled back around the dreaded question.

"Why are you here today?" She looked concerned, sad, and professional, trying to make sense of the nurse's notes.

I answered her questions. No symptoms. No changes. No outbreaks.

She recommended a full panel of testing. One prick. Lots of blood. And many tests. She rattled off the names of every STD this panel would test for. I waited until I heard the name of the one I knew I needed to be tested for.

I agreed to the testing and walked down the hall to the lab. After a few more minutes of waiting, my name was called again.

The lab tech wore her gloves on and asked, "Do you know what you're being tested for?"

Why are these people so darn thorough?!

"Yes," I answered.

She proceeded to list off the names of the STDs I had heard moments prior from my doctor.

"Is this correct?"

"Unfortunately… I mean, yes, it is."

I also wanted to say, "Please lower your voice! There is no need to alert the entire building of my testing!"

A small amount of my blood was taken to fill several vials for testing, but I already knew so much more had been taken from me. I didn't have the test results, but I wanted to crawl under my covers and never return to society.

I walked out of the lab, weak and lifeless.

Why did you sleep with him?!

How could you be so stupid? So irresponsible!

This will ruin your life.

No one will ever love you again.

So much for freedom. So much for healing.

The moment I slid into the driver's seat, gut-wrenching sobs escaped from my chest. Excruciating pain crashed upon my heart.

And I was afraid. Afraid of what people would think of me. Afraid of what people would say. I was afraid everything I did and everything I touched would be plagued by a diagnosis.

A week later, I received the results.

Positive. Incurable.

"I still love you."

I'm finding that a little hard to believe right now, Lord.

Have you ever had a moment like this? Questioning God's love for you. You're questioning God's love because you believe He was the giver. Someone had to give us this bag, right? And it's definitely not something we would give ourselves. So, naturally, a lot of us blame The Healer for whatever bag we got.

Nevermind all the personal choices we made along the way. Forget all the warning signs. The red flags. We take no responsibility for this. Instead, we blame God.

Or the pendulum of blame swings and crashes into ourselves. We are questioning God's love because we don't even love ourselves. We are disgusted with ourselves. We are ashamed of the outcome. We are desperately trying to bury the evidence of our bag. Therefore, there is absolutely zero chance God can love us right now.

Praise God; His love isn't conditional or situational. Praise God; He still loves us despite our attempts to cast blame. Praise God; His love supersedes all shame we ignorantly cling to.

We see God's unconditional love in the book of Genesis. The Lord is calling out to Adam, asking where he is. Adam and Eve had just eaten from the tree God specifically told them not to. God had given them so much freedom and opportunity everywhere else in the Garden of Eden, but He gave them this boundary not to eat from the tree of the knowledge of good and evil (see Genesis 2:15-17).

In chapter 3 verse 10, Adam replies, "I heard Your voice in the garden, and I was afraid because I was naked; and I hid myself." In verse 11, God answers, "Who told you that you were naked?" (New King James Version)

Adam messed up and became afraid. He knew the boundary God placed before him. He knew it was a mistake. He knew there would be consequences.

The crazy part of this story is that he heard God's voice. He knew the Lord was looking for Him. He knew the Lord was searching for him. He knew the Lord was concerned and cared for him. But instead of running towards his Father, The Healer, he hid because of shame.

When I read verse 11, I see God's heart hurting for Adam and Eve. I hear His voice breaking when He asks Adam, "Who told you that you were naked?"

Who placed shame on you? Who told you to hide? Who told you to be afraid? Who told you you were a mistake? Who told you you were worthless? Who told you you were incurable? Who told you you were unlovable? Who told you that you were naked?

Who told you?

In those moments when we don't have control. When it's something we can't fix. When we are utterly helpless. He still loves us. When shame is silencing us. When fear suffocates. When the unknowns keep mounting, and you're already dreading tomorrow... He still loves us.

He's still searching for us. He's still concerned about us. He still cares for us.

"

Who told you?

"

This was the worst bag I could have been given! Y'all, I got the empty-no-healing-incurable-STD bag.

Does anyone want to trade? No? No takers?

I would never switch this bag with anyone, but I also definitely didn't want it. I would have loved to trade this bag in, or ,at the very least, pretend it wasn't mine.

But pretending doesn't prevent reality. Every choice has its consequences. We see this with Adam and Eve as well. The Lord still loved them, but there were consequences to the broken boundaries. There were consequences to my choices as well. I had to be completely honest with myself. These were my choices. Albeit poor ones, but my choices nonetheless.

Some of us didn't get to choose what happened to us. Some things were forced upon us, stolen from us, and withheld from us.

But this was my reality. I didn't outright choose infection or disease. But I did choose other things.

Things I had to come to terms with:

— The Lord did not make me date him. I chose to date him.

— The Lord did not make me have sex. I chose to have sex.

— The Lord did not make me stay in that relationship. I chose to stay.

— The Lord wasn't punishing me. I was punishing myself.

— The Lord wasn't saying, "I told you so." I was shaming myself with that phrase.

> **Pretending doesn't prevent reality.**

The Lord wasn't shaming me or guilting me. He wasn't flashing all my screw-ups on a big screen. I was doing that to myself.

I was the one discounting myself based on the diagnosis. I was the one screaming, "This doesn't happen to people like me (...check out the stats,

Court)!" I just knew no one would understand. No one would ever love me, let alone respect me. If I told anyone, all they would see is STD Courtney, plagued with disease. A social pariah. They wouldn't get close. They definitely wouldn't touch. They'd be afraid of infection. They'd wonder if I was contagious, only interact from afar, and never get too close.

The psychological war invaded my brain. Crusading every crevice. Threatening to take territory daily.

The onslaught had to cease. I wanted to move forward, but I kept clinging to the past. I kept identifying with the diagnosis. I thought if I still had even one tie to the past, I couldn't possess the future the Lord had for me. I believed that as long as I tested positive, I was ruined and worthless. I denied any good and discounted any redeemable qualities within me because, in my mind, I didn't deserve them. I deserved to suffer for my choices.

This psychological skirmish was impeding my healing process. Sadness consumed me. I didn't want to tell people about my diagnosis, but I wanted them to know my sadness. I wanted them to know the agony I was experiencing. I wore sadness like a cloak. It draped over my shoulders, sunk into my eyes, and withered my heart.

If this is you. If this is what you're experiencing right now. I say this with all the tenderness I can…

Eventually, you have to get past looking for sympathy and start finding solutions.

The Lord was offering me a path of healing. One that would make me whole regardless of a doctor's script. Regardless of a test. Regardless of medicine. Regardless of what others said to my face or behind my back. It was an invitation to embrace a healing I'd never experienced before.

If I truly believed the Lord was good and that He wasn't a liar, then I couldn't believe He gave me this diagnosis. I had to choose to believe Romans 8:28, "And we know that for those who love God all things work together for good, for those who are called according to his purpose" (New King James Version). There was no magical bag of diagnosis or healing that I was arbitrarily given. And no, I cannot explain why certain things happen to some people and certain things don't happen to others. But what I could believe was that the Lord was good and that He wanted good for my life.

I had a choice to make. And so do you.

Will you let what happened to you define you or refine you? Will you allow the Lord to mend you, assemble your broken pieces, diagnosis, and all? Will you choose healing?

I chose yes, and I have never regretted it. Not one second of any day.

Sometimes, life turns out differently than we had planned. Sneaky sabotage. Debilitating diagnosis. Rock-bottom betrayal. All of which cannot be wished away, changed, or rewritten. We don't get to exchange the original bag we were handed (sticking with the original metaphor). But we can learn how to redeem our future when the past cannot be changed.

So, if you want to choose healing, read on.

Not So Fun Facts:

— Over half of the people in the U.S. will have an STI, other than HIV, at some point in their lifetime.[1]

— Most common STDs include HPV, genital herpes, trichomoniasis, and chlamydia.

---

1 kff.org

— Preliminary data show 2.5 million reported cases of chlamydia, gonorrhea, and syphilis in 2021 (Centers for Disease Control and Prevention).

— More than 1 million STIs are acquired daily worldwide, most of which are asymptomatic. [2]

Pause:

_____

_____

_____

_____

_____

Ponder:

1. What psychological war games are you playing and replaying in your mind?

_____

_____

_____

_____

_____

---

2   World Health Organization

2. What do you believe about healing? Where do you struggle with healing?

_____

_____

_____

_____

_____

Prayer:

Lord, I pray my friend receives your personal invitation towards healing. Regardless of the bag they were given, I pray they are open and receptive to the healing journey you are inviting them on. I pray the psychological war games must cease TODAY in the name of Jesus. That they will release guilt and shame and that they will exchange it for peace of mind. In John 14:27, you said, "I am leaving you with a gift—peace of mind and heart. And the peace I give is a gift the world cannot give. So don't be troubled or afraid." I pray they will quit beating themselves up for the things in the past and that they will accept your invitation to redeem our past by redefining our future. Amen.

_____

_____

_____

_____

_____

Chapter Eight

Healing Isn't Linear

The first time I processed the words, "Healing isn't linear," I was in a session with my life coach. We had discussed the idea that motherhood's success isn't linear (an entirely different topic for a different book), and I had this revelation that healing isn't linear either. We were discussing how my book writing was going, and I mentioned I was struggling with writing certain chapters because I was reliving the pain, the trauma, and the grief all over again. Things I thought I healed from were rearing their ugly head again.

> **Healing isn't linear.**

Healing isn't linear.

Let me break it down.

Somewhere along the way, we convinced ourselves that there is an appropriate timeline and a proper progression for healing. That by this x amount of time, we should be x amount healed. We have to keep moving forward. Keep healing. Otherwise, we are failing. We are allowed to experience the pain, the trauma, and the grief but only in a specific season, and if you experience any or all outside of that sacred season, there is something wrong with you.

My friend, I would like to call this ideology a number of names, but we will stick with what my late Grandma Betty referred to as hogwash. Nonsense if you will. Grandma Betty retorted, "Hogwash" when something was incredulous. Something did not fit, did not match, did not make sense. It was absurd, it was outlandish, and it was false.

Many of our perspectives of healing are just that. Absurd. Outlandish. False. We have grabbed onto notions from society to tell us when we should be "over" something. We have listened to emotionally unstable and similarly emotionally unpredictable family members telling us to move on or that our healing has to look a certain way. We have clung to spiritual cliches that our faith isn't strong enough, sin is in our lives, or if it's not immediate, it won't happen.

Don't throw stones just yet... I believe in strong faith. I believe an unexamined life is not worth living (thank you, Socrates). And I do believe in immediate supernatural healing. But healing is a topic that could cover several books instead of just a couple of chapters. But the conversation needs to start here and now. I can't wait for the next book to give you all the details on healing. I can't give you all the Scriptures, all the podcasts, or all the book suggestions. I'll let you do further research, but what I can do is talk to you from personal experience.

My sister eloquently stated, "Healing is unique like a finger-print." So, it's okay if your healing doesn't look like someone else's. Personally, I like to exhaustively talk through my issues to find healing. My sister doesn't want to talk at first. She'd rather destroy people in Jiu-Jitsu. If I did Jiu-Jitsu, I'd cry and have more healing to work through–physically and emotionally.

While we both understand we cannot just workout and avoid our problems, we also recognize that we don't heal identically. She doesn't heal like me, and I don't heal like her. It's just a part of who we are. We are both unique, just like our fingerprints.

So, I can tell you it's okay if you're still struggling. It's okay if you thought you had it together one day, and the next, you're falling apart. It's okay if you hadn't cried for a month, and then you cried daily for a week.

It's okay if you miss the good conversations. The sound of their voice. The familiar touch. The scent of the apartment. It's okay if you think about going back... again.

Too real?

It's okay if you stand in the shower and weep until your knees give out. It's okay if you sob until you gasp for air. Sometimes, grief feels like death.

It's okay if you're confused. Where it once scared and scarred you, now you want the embrace of familiarity. It's hard to com-prehend because a lot was bad. But some things were good. It truly was good. It's okay to grieve what was and what could have been.

It's okay if you want to box, run, or swim to find some solace, but please don't rely solely on physical exertion. It's okay if you need individual or group counseling. It's okay if you need a support group or all three at once.

The pain, the trauma, and the grief complicate healing. Sometimes, you make massive strides forward. Other times, you're looping back around, thanks to a trigger. One step back. Three steps forward. Hop to the left. Lean to the right. It's like calisthenics for healing.

Allow me to share this with you.

The maybe not-so-great news- it's a never-ending process.

The good news—it's a never-ending process.

The best news- it's a never-ending process.

Like we cycled through hope in Chapter 5, we cycle through healing. When we ask ourselves, "Why am I still struggling?" that indicates a battle is raging. A war is being had. Something or someone is trying to take your ground. So, we have the opportunity to combat the struggle and claim the healing that is rightfully ours. We have the authority to stand firm.

Friend, hold your ground. Don't give up. You're worth the effort. Put in the work.

Late renowned scientist and Nobel Prize winner Marie Curie, said, "Nothing is to be feared, only understood." When you feel that twinge of pain or a traumatic memory, do not fear. This is an opportunity to understand why it still has a hold on you. Where the strongholds tampered with your soul, so shall healing. Healing must make its way and take up residence in those areas in desperate need of the Holy Spirit's touch.

> **Friend, hold your ground. Don't give up. You're worth the effort. Put in the work.**

We *get* to work on our healing. We *get* to learn and understand ourselves more. And each time we walk (or crawl) through part of the healing process, we can find another level of confidence and empowerment. We learn that those things, moments, and people are not what defines us. They don't get to hold us back any longer. They don't get to keep us from our new beginning. We have opportunities to let go of things that have been weighing us down, and we will have moments when we get to share our healing with others and encourage them that it is possible.

These are four steps that I have taken and continue to take on my "healing isn't linear" journey. I circle through and through these three areas continuously. They help me navigate life and stay the course to find new levels of healing.

Get grounded- Get grounded has two parts to it. The first part is grounding into our basic needs, and the second part is grounding ourselves in faith. Per psychology, I believe we have to tackle the first part of grounding before we can address the second part.

First Part- Hello Maslow.

Do you remember psychology class and Maslow's hierarchy of needs? If not, let me take you back to class. Abraham Maslow and his famous triangle. Basically, you start at the bottom of the triangle and have to work your way up. You can't skip steps on the triangle; you can only move up once you have previously satisfied the needs. Here's a breakdown of the triangle thanks to Platerseca/ Getty Images (https://www.thoughtco.com/maslows-hierarchy-of-needs-4582571).

Figure 1: Maslow's hierarchy of needs (Maslow 1943)

Many who have left an abusive or toxic relationship are starting at the bottom of Maslow's triangle. We have basic needs that we have to meet before we can ever talk about building up our self-esteem and becoming the best version of ourselves. Status is great, but not when we are concerned about shelter and food. So, first, we have to identify where we are in order to meet our needs. And if we are responsible for children, it's hard for us to move up the triangle if we haven't met their needs as well.

Maslow's hierarchy of needs is a great stepping stone for all of us to know where we are currently and where we are going (toxic relationships or not). Then we can form a plan to continue to satisfy needs and move up the triangle. We have to alleviate any perceived scarcity or lack of safety before we move into the second part.

**Please approach getting grounded with compassion and curiosity. Wherever you're starting, the point is that you are starting! You're beginning again, and that is a beautiful and honorable feat.

Second Part- Hello Jesus.

What are you standing on? What are you anchored to? I used to be grounded in the grief of my past. That was the only thing I clung to. Those were the only records I rehearsed. Day in and day out, I anchored myself in shame and guilt. So, naturally, my current state of life was filled with shame and guilt. That wasn't healing, and it wasn't working.

I switched tactics and decided that I would no longer root myself in shame and guilt. I needed to stand on the truth. I needed to be anchored to something bigger than myself. Something (or someone) that could hold the weight of my shame and guilt. Someone who would continuously remind me that I am not my mistakes. I am not my past. Someone who would give me hope.

I became grounded in the words Jesus speaks over all of us, and if we embrace the hope and truth He offers, the trajectory of our lives will dramatically (and positively) change.

"I praise you because I am fearfully and wonderfully made; your works are wonderful, I know that full well." Psalms 139:14

I still recite this Scripture over myself because I have this unfortunate ability to scrutinize all my achievements, abilities, and attributes. If there was a trophy for who could tear apart their self-worth the fastest, I'm pretty sure I'd win. So, if you're anything like me, you have to squash the scrutiny with Scripture.

We were crafted, each one of us, with unique wonder. The Lord took time to individually fill in our idiosyncrasies, features, personality, and preferences. There is only one of each of us. He did not create us to be like anyone else. The only person He created us in a similar fashion to was Himself. He made us in His likeness. He did an amazing job creating you and me. We are wonderful, and we have to keep reciting that and proclaiming that over our lives until we believe it.

Write it on your bathroom mirror. Hang it from your rearview mirror. Set a recurring reminder on your phone. Whatever works for you, do it! Read it daily. Multiple times a day until they aren't just words you say but truth flowing from your heart.

66

We were crafted, each one of us, with unique wonder.

99

I then exchanged shame and guilt for hope and a future. Jeremiah 29:11 says, "For I know the plans I have for you, declares the Lord, plans to prosper you and not to harm you, plans to give you hope and a future" (New International Version).

I used to be so frustrated—irate even when people would quote this Scripture. I was so mad hearing Jeremiah 29:11 because my life was in shambles. They would quote those words, and under my breath and in my heart, I thought...

What type of plan is this God? My life is terrible!

The only thing prospering in my life is drama.

Plans not to harm me? I've been hurt plenty of times, and the damage continues.

What is hope? I have none of that.

Not only did I hard-core roll my eyes at this Scripture, but I never thought it possible for my life. I didn't think it could be true. That was my belief, and that was my reality. And I truly believe you'll only go as far as you can believe. One day, instead of being disgusted with this particular Scripture, I decided to get curious. What if it were true? What if it were possible? What if I could get past my pain and hope again? What would my future hold?

And I can tell you with certainty that the Lord has never let me down. He's never abandoned me. He's never left me. He's never hurt me. I may wander, but He never does. I may grow cold or silent, but He remains steadfast, unchanging, and always loving.

66

You'll only go as far as you can believe.

I started memorizing Scripture that spoke to my situation. I wrote them out on notecards and recited them daily, sometimes multiple times a day. I replaced rehearsing my pain with rehearsing truth, hope, and love. I read the Scriptures until they weren't just words on a card but truth etched on my heart. Until I knew I embodied those words, I lived out those words. I believed those words. I could see them in action in my life.

Getting grounded in the Bible will strengthen your faith. It will increase your hope. It will brighten your future. It will challenge your perception. I started reworking things I previously believed about myself. I challenged fallacies from my past and explored what life could be like if I were completely healthy, happy, and whole. I continued to believe all of those things until I saw them come to fruition in my life.

Crack open a Bible or a Bible app, or even search Scripture online. Find a handful that resonates with you, your situation, and what you believe for your healing, life, and future. Read them until you believe them. Then find more Scriptures and go again.

Get generous- Get generous with yourself! I learned this concept from Brene Brown's books. She talked about giving the most generous assumption to someone else. For example, when your sister is notorious for running late and yet again she is not on time for your brunch date, instead of getting annoyed and angry, you give her the most generous assumption. In those moments (hypothetically speaking, of course), I give her the most generous assumption that she is running late because her morning was crazy, and she is doing her best to honor and respect our brunch date. Almost always, I feel the tension lessen and the peace return when I believe someone is doing the absolute best they can.

Now, we must start being generous with ourselves! You are doing the best you can right now with the resources you have! Blaming ourselves for not seeing "it" sooner does not help the situation, and I can promise that it will impede the healing process.

When you go on the roller coaster of emotions and don't know how to handle the rage, give yourself space and understanding to feel, accept, and express.

When you've gone down the dark rabbit hole trying to connect all the dots of their misdeeds and deception, give yourself grace. Pull yourself out of the tunnel and release the never-ending loops of lies.

When you find yourself in the trance of twisting your hair, pinching your skin, plucking your lashes, chewing your nails, picking at your skin, biting your lip, or whatever your trauma response is, please be kind to yourself. These behaviors and habits are indicators that something has triggered you. You might be feeling anxious, out of control, stressed, unsafe, or a myriad of other emotions. Whatever the case, this is an opportunity for you to first be generously kind to yourself and secondly to move into curiosity.

So, when the barrage of belittling comments swarm your brain, battle them with Truth. Ask yourself, "What is true about this situation? What are the facts? What does God say about me?" The more you consistently reframe, challenge, and debunk, the quieter and less frequent the lies become.

Your healing journey will be unique. There will be victories. There will be setbacks. Be generous and be kind to yourself. Give yourself permission to not have it all together. Give yourself permission to keep healing. Give yourself permission to learn about yourself and the God who wonderfully and masterfully created you.

When the barrage of belittling comments swarm your brain, battle them with Truth.

Get curious- Ask really good

questions. The more you practice asking questions, the better your questions become. You can begin by asking yourself some of these starter questions.

The Questions

— What am I feeling?

— What is under this emotion/action/thought?

— Is this emotion/action/thought connected to something?

— Is there something I need to let go of?

— Is there something I haven't addressed?

— Is there something I need to readdress?

After sifting through the questions and gaining awareness of the situation, now is the time to establish some boundaries.

The Boundaries

Remember Lysa's book and Dr. Cloud's book? Seriously, go check them out. I also like the term guardrails. Andy Stanley uses it in his Bible study entitled Guardrails. He says the purpose of guardrails is to keep us from going into the ditch. We don't want to be in the ditch. Hitting the ditch causes so much damage and many problems.

If you hit a guardrail, however, it can still be painful but less destructive. The guardrail is there to protect you from going into the ditch. It keeps you centered on your side of the road. It gives you boundaries to know where it is acceptable to drive and where it is not. If you start to veer off towards a guardrail, you'll usually hit the rumble strips first. This abrupt, noisy warning is disrupts your usual flow, indicating you're drifting away from the safe zone.

We need guardrails in our lives to keep us from steering down or back down the path of destruction. We need guardrails for ourselves and in our dealings with others. Continuing with the metaphor of a guardrail, I envision what the perfect road looks like for me. I see Maslow's Hierarchy, and I get curious. If this is what the perfect road looks like specifically for me, then what guardrails do I need to put in place? What would be the ditch I don't want to end up in?

I cannot answer those questions for you, but I do pray you get curious, assess, and implement. Then reassess, make changes where necessary, and implement again. Give yourself permission to keep learning. To keep assessing. And to keep improving.

On a practical note: At the end of every month, I assess where I'm at with my goals, my boundaries, my relationships, etc. I reassess where I went off course, make changes, and implement new boundaries and strategies where necessary. Then, once every quarter, I do this again but much deeper. I assess every facet of my life. I have people in my life to speak into these areas (See the Get Surrounded part further down).

Mark those days on your calendar. It doesn't have to be a long, drawn-out process, but it helps keep you consistent and steady. I highly recommend this practice.

The Game

The last part of getting curious requires us to play a little game. Remember the game Two Truths And A Lie? I despised this game because I was no good at it. I couldn't make my lie convincing enough. I didn't know how to make it blend in with the two truths, and I couldn't distinguish between the two truths and the lie others shared. Some people were so good at disguising their lies! It all sounded true to me! Seriously. I believed all three statements every time, so it was just a shot in the dark guessing what didn't fit. I knew this particular game meant there had to be a lie hidden amongst the truth, but I couldn't pin-point the deception. It was so frustrating, and I always lost.

My friend, in this game of life, there is a real enemy (Satan) trying to convince you of his lies. Unfortunately, he doesn't have to work very hard because we believe all his statements as truth when in reality they are lies! We must get better at distinguishing the lies. Pin-pointing and addressing the deception. He does not get to harbor his lies in our hearts any longer.

With total honesty, I have sat down in a belief battle desperately asking, "What is the lie, and what is the truth?" I asked myself, "What are the facts?" Sometimes, I have even written out what I'm thinking or what someone has said about me. Then, I determine again where the lies end and the truth begins.

You see, friend, lies corrupt our true Kingdom identity. When we believe the terrible things said about or done to us, or even the thoughts we've conjured up in our own minds, we relinquish our rights as heirs to a Kingdom. And, of course, the enemy wants us to think his lies are true. Then we don't enjoy any of the benefits of being sons and daughters of a King. We believe we are lowly, less than, and left out. The lies steal and scorch the Truth.

Lies will always leave you feeling or believing less than about yourself. Lies will never lead you toward goodness. Lies will always discount your worth. Lies will always downplay your input, your value, and your intellect. Lies will always put you down, leave you insecure, and trample on your dreams.

The Truth will always leave you feeling and believing better things about yourself. The truth is life-giving and up-lifting. The Truth will lead you toward goodness and godliness. The Truth will illuminate your worth. The Truth will empower you to share your input, protect your value, and respect your intellect. The Truth will always build you up, leave you stronger, and propel you toward your God-given dreams.

This is why it is vital that we identify the lies that have corrupted our Kingdom identity and replace them with the Truth. Because the truth is you are more valuable than rubies, you are marked for greatness, and you are worth all this great effort!

Get surrounded- I firmly believe that who you surround yourself with, you will become. I also believe you teach others how to treat you by what you allow, what you stop, and what you reinforce. From experience, ignoring will not eliminate or alleviate; it escalates and perpetuates. You have to have the hard conversations with yourself and sometimes others especially if it makes you uncomfortable.

So here are some more tough questions to consider.

— Who are you spending your time with? How do they influence you?

— Who are you letting speak into your life?

— What do you listen to? Watch? Read?

— What do you meditate on? Pray for?

— When you're alone, what does that voice in your head tell you about you?

— Answer those questions and move on to this next set.

— Now that you know your guardrails, goals, ditches, etc., and have answered the above questions, who should still influence your life? Who should not?

— Who should be speaking into your life? What do you want them to say?

— What do you need to stop listening to, watching, or reading? What do you need to start listening to, watching, or reading?

— What mantras or prayers should you be reciting?

— What would you like to be able to say about yourself?

— What would you like others to be able to say about you?

The answers to these questions will help navigate who and what you need to be surrounded by. If you're not already, start attending a faith-filled church regularly. This will make it easier when I suggest… get involved at said church. Getting involved at church might look like taking notes during the service, joining a community/small/grow group (whatever they call it), serving, etc.

Getting surrounded might mean more in-depth healing with a therapist. Or it might be a specific program through a non-profit or through that aforementioned church. I promise you that the resources for healing are out there. You just have to ask and research.

Lastly and most importantly, surround yourself with Jesus. When you answered the questions and realized, oh shoot, I need some new friends… or oh shoot, I need friends. Pray! Pray for Godly friends and influences. People you can trust. People who have your best interests at heart. People who will hold you accountable and healthily love you through this journey. Jesus might be your only best friend until those prayers are answered, and from firsthand experience, He's an amazing best friend who will never let you down.

Pause:

_____

_____

_____

_____

_____

Ponder:

1. What did you learn about healing in this chapter?

_____

_____

_____

_____

_____

2. What are you going to implement to further your healing journey?

_____

_____

_____

_____

_____

Prayer:

Lord, I pray my friend gives themselves grace on this healing journey. I pray they will be kind to themselves as they navigate victories, setbacks, and stalemates on this road. Please make abundantly clear what guardrails should be implemented in their life. Help them commit to getting grounded, generous, curious, and surrounded. I pray Jeremiah 29:11 fills their soul with hope and that they believe there is a great future ahead of them. Thank you for being their best friend every step of the way. We love you!

_____

_____

_____

_____

_____

Chapter Nine

My Life Matters

Afew weeks prior to writing this chapter, I struggled
with depression and anxiety. And when I say struggled, I mean like I'm-trying-to-make-it-through-the-
next-few-hours type of struggle. I'd go to sleep, already dreading the next morning.

This battle went on for months. I was constantly tired, and
even though I was exhausted, I wasn't getting restful sleep. The
intrusive thoughts were debilitating. I couldn't write. I didn't
exercise. It was agonizing to do basic everyday chores like grocery shopping or even making my bed.

Here, I was almost ten years removed from an abusive relationship. Now I'm in a healthy and thriving Godly marriage with
a beautiful toddler, and I couldn't see the next day. My church

was amazing. My friends were like family.

I even reread the Healing Isn't Linear chapter to remind myself to keep going. To keep being generous with myself, to keep my curiosity sparked, and to stay surrounded by Godly influences.

So, how on earth, or better yet, why on earth was I struggling?

John 10:10 says, "The thief does not come except to steal, and to kill, and to destroy. I have come that they may have life, and that they may have it more abundantly" (New King James Version).

I agonized over how to finish these last few chapters when I was in such a rough spot. How can I send you out on a high note when I was in the trenches myself?

I had an epiphany that the enemy knew the greatness these chapters would hold. The breakthrough this book would bring. The healing. The hope. The salvations. And he was doing everything in his power to steal my peace, kill my dreams, and destroy this book.

He didn't want me to keep going on. He didn't want me to finish. He wanted to remind me of every failure from my past, every time I didn't write, and of every time I didn't do something right. He tried to use every tactic, every insecurity, and every flaw to make me quit.

I almost gave up. I was so tired of fighting each day. I was running on fumes and didn't know if I had the strength or really the desire to keep going. It's wild to think he almost won.

It wasn't until a discerning, God-fearing sister in Christ prayed the spirit of torment out of and off of my life that I started to think and see clearly. Ever since that holy encounter, my mind has been free. The spirit of slumber was removed. The intrusive thoughts were silenced.

The energy, passion, and gratitude… it all came flowing back. I remember waking up one day and realizing how much I love my life. How thankful I am for my life. How blessed I am to live this life.

And as I was spending time with the Lord, I kept hearing, "My life matters."

There were moments in my past abusive relationships where I did not believe my life mattered. The way I was talked to, talked about, and the way I was treated. It didn't matter. I didn't matter.

And now, many moons removed from those situations, I was still battling whether my life mattered, but the Holy Spirit was so sweet to remind me that I do matter. My life matters. And I know now why I went through those months.

I was battling for you.

The Holy Spirit spoke that over me, but not just for me. He spoke it so clearly and intimately that I could speak it over you today.

Your life matters!

Right here. Right now. Your life matters. Not just when you're healthy. Not just when you're in therapy. Not just when you're nice to your kids. Not just when you are on cloud nine.

Your life matters!

"

Your life matters!

"

Suicidal or not. Self-harming or not. Still in that relationship or not. Your life matters here and now. No matter what state of mind you're in. No matter your physical, financial, emotional, or spiritual state.

Your life matters!

Some of you have believed everything I've said up to this point, but now you don't know if you can buy into this. Some of you are thinking about just hiding in the shadows and laying low. Out of sight, out of mind.

Some of you are stuck in the nobody mentality. You think of yourself as a nobody. You think you are not important. Nobody knows me. Nobody wants to know me. Nobody will listen. Nobody will care. Nobody will miss me.

And I'm here to tell you that NOBODY has told you that except an enemy trying to steal, kill, and destroy.

The enemy wants you to just get by. He wants you to simply cope and coast through your days. He hopes you read this book and do nothing about it. He wants you to walk away simply saying, "Oh, wow, that was nice," and then go about your life with zero change. He needs you to forget the action steps, skip the homework, and discount yourself.

He wants to remind you of your faults, flaws, and failures. He will poke and nag and prod at you like he did me. He will bring up past wounds. He will try to uncover old scars. He will change tactics and come from different angles, desperate to keep you quiet and to make you quit.

Why? Because he fears what can happen when you take action. He fears what whole-hearted change will look like within you. He fears what will happen when you start believing and acting like your life matters.

He is frightened by the potential you possess. He squirms, knowing how connection and community will spark an unquenchable joy deep within your bones.

You must resist reclusivity. Don't shrink back or shy away. Don't retreat. Don't withdraw.

Withdrawing with purpose has its seasons. Luke 5:16 says, "So He Himself often withdrew into the wilderness and prayed" (New King James Version). Jesus withdrew with a purpose—a healthy intent. He didn't withdraw to avoid people or run away. He withdrew in order to reconnect. He reconnected with the Father, and then He went back out to reconnect with people.

His withdrawal wasn't for isolation. It was for connection, and it was for relationships.

I want you to soar, sing, and belly laugh. I want your eyes to light up with excitement again!

Who are you going to listen to? Is it an enemy that is ready to steal, kill, and destroy? Or the Holy Spirit who is sweetly saying, *"Your life matters?"*

Make a choice right now. At this very moment, as you are reading these paragraphs, declare that your life matters!

After I left my abusive relationship, I believed my life mattered and what I did next would change the trajectory of my future. So, I took inventory.

I took inventory of habits, thoughts, behaviors, and beliefs I had of myself and others. I took inventory of my likes and dislikes. I was trying to figure out who I was and, more so, who I wanted to be. I sifted carefully and compassionately, recognizing what habits I did not want to take with me in this next phase of life. And I chose what I wanted to take with me.

For example, I realized I was extremely angry. Like 0 to 100 duck and cover, Courtney is coming through. Screaming, yelling, verbally nasty, angry. I didn't like it. I didn't want to be that way, but it just erupted out of me.

I decided that instead of being known to erupt like a volcano and scorch all those in proximity, I wanted to be known as someone full of joy and peace.

Y'all, that's a full flip.

I learned coping mechanisms when I got angry. I found the triggers to my anger. I did the homework I suggested to you in each and every chapter. And the crazy thing is that the more I read the Word, the more I thought and responded like Christ. When I tell people now that I had an anger problem, they look confused. When I tell people, I used to scream and yell when in fights, they think I'm lying.

Why? Because they see the change. They see joy and peace.

I can't say I woke up one morning and never said another curse word again in my life. I can't say I never lost my temper. And I can't say that everyone who encounters me experiences joy and peace. But I can tell you they see more joy and peace now than they would have seen in me last year and the year before that and the year before that.

It's a process, and it's progress. And I am committed to believing that improving my life matters.

So, what fulfills you? What makes you happy? What do you enjoy doing?

Some of you might not know. You might not even remember, and that's okay! You get to discover who you are now. You get to dive in, try new things, make new memories, and experiment with hobbies until you find one that clicks!

66

Finding out who you are and investing in you is the greatest adventure if you'll allow it to be.

99

Finding out who you are and investing in you is the greatest adventure if you'll allow it to be.

Start dreaming again! Your dreams, your desires, and your

ambitions are not silly. And you are not an inconvenience. Pouring into you will be the best decision you've ever made for you and your family (present and future).

So, let's start pouring! Listed below are several exercises I use to remind myself that my life matters. I use different exercises depending on my season of life and where I am mentally.

Think of these like accessories (and if you're not into fashion, think of the same concept but with tools and a toolbelt). Sometimes I wear earrings, a watch, a necklace, sunglasses and a handbag. Other times, I'm keepin' it simple with my wedding rings. I have access to all my accessories, but I choose what to wear based on the occasion at hand. The season. The company. Sometimes, I look back over my jewelry box and remind myself what I have at my disposal. I exchange pieces in and out and add new pieces to my collection. I even retire pieces when necessary.

So pick and choose. You might not need some of these accessories right now, or you might need several. And it's okay if you need them all!

I Sense A Mantra

What do you need to tell yourself? A mantra is usually short, so it's easily memorable and memorizable, and it either positively speaks to who you currently are, or it embodies who you are becoming.

I am grateful for my health and life coach certification from the Health Coach Institute (HCI). Their training has equipped and empowered me to create and anchor mantras like the one below.

For example, when I started working out again after having my daughter, I had immense mom guilt. I was investing in myself, but I felt so bad for leaving her with someone else. So, I created a mantra.

Every time I left to go to the gym, I'd look at my daughter and say, "I'm going to take care of myself, so I can come back and take care of you." This mantra released me from my guilt and allowed me to fully focus on my workout.

My favorite part about mantras is anchoring them with our senses. Think of your five senses (smell, touch, sight, taste, sound). When you pair your mantra with a five-sense anchor, it helps ground you even more.

From the workout example, I had a specific perfume I sprayed before I went to the gym. I'd say the mantra to myself as I sprayed the perfume. Then on the way out the door, I'd repeat the mantra to my daughter. Every time I'd get a whiff of the perfume, it would remind me of my mantra and keep me anchored to the goal at hand.

Anchor Ideas:

Smell- candle, perfume, lotion, toothpaste, body wash/scrub, cleaning supplies

Touch- comfy blanket, pillow, stress ball, fidget device

Sight- certain color, sticky note, framed picture, note on mirror, poem, book

Taste- a mint, gum, a drink

Sound- a song, birds chirping, humming, phone alert/chime/ding

These are a mere handful of ideas. Use some of these or add on with your own! You decide what anchors you'd like! You can change them or switch them up whenever you'd like. They are yours to utilize.

Now, use the three steps below to put your mantras into place.

Step One: What do you need to tell yourself? Write it down.

Step Two: Which five senses do you want to pair it with? What does that look like for you?

Step Three: When will you say your mantra out loud with your anchor?

Mirror Mirror

What are the mantras you are declaring? Do you have a mirror? You're set. Stand in front of the mirror and for 5 minutes repeat your mantra. Look yourself in the eye, and repeat your mantra. Say it until you believe it. Say it until your confidence rises. Say it every day until it becomes who you are.

Forewarning: I usually end up crying doing the Mirror Mirror exercise. Especially when my mantra was looking into the mirror and saying, "I love you," over and over and over until I truly believed I loved that girl staring back at me in the mirror.

So, my advice is to have some tissues nearby.

Hard No's

I implemented Hard No's into my life after my abusive relationship. This was specifically in regards to dating, but you can do this for any area in your life. Hard No's were characteristics, traits, etc., in a man that were non-negotiable. If they possessed or portrayed those traits, I couldn't consider them an option for dating.

Before you throw stones, hold up. It didn't mean they were a bad person. I believe everyone is made in the image of God, but it did mean that I had specific standards and values. I wanted the other person to value, treasure, and cherish what I valued, treasured, and cherished. I needed clear-cut expectations and standards to sift through the possible options.

And guess what? It was hard! I turned down dates. You do not have to answer every text, DM, or phone call. It is okay to delete without responding. You are in charge of your Hard No's and your boundaries.

I didn't want to date for the sake of dating anymore. I wanted the next person I dated to be my husband. I wasn't messing around or playing games. And I certainly wasn't repeating my past.

And guess what? My next boyfriend became my husband and the amazing father to our daughter. All those "no's" before Grant made saying "yes" to him so incredibly sweet.

You can implement Hard No's for jobs, family reunions, friendships, etc. There are certain things you will not consider for your next job. There are certain people you will not associate with at the reunion. There are certain characteristics you will not tolerate in a friend. You get my drift, right?

My husband and I are currently looking for a new vehicle, and I despise car shopping. So, we implemented Hard No's. For example, it was a Hard No for us if it wasn't all-wheel drive or four-wheel drive. Salesmen would bring a vehicle through the lot, and we said no if it didn't have either of those features. They would implore us to just sit in the seats or take a look at the numbers, and again, we would say no.

I'm not going to entertain an idea that crosses my Hard No. I have that boundary in place for a reason, so I do not settle for less than what I originally wanted. So, yes, we have had to say "no" many times, and that is okay! Because we know that eventually, we'll be able to say "yes," and it will be so sweet.

UPDATE Since writing those aforementioned paragraphs,

we said yes to our vehicle, and she (yes, my SUV is a girl) was worth every single Hard No we said prior!

Life Enhancers

I came up with the term "Life Enhancers" after my abusive relationship as well, and I continue to implement this even in my marriage today. Life Enhancers were things I wanted to personally work on (i.e., being a better listener, respecting others' opinions, complimenting others more, etc.). I was not a healthy person in my abusive relationship or after that relationship for that matter.

I was not a good candidate for dating, let alone marriage. Life Enhancers gave me a vision for the person I wanted to become. It showed me the end result of who I desired to be, and then I worked on becoming that desired woman of God. You can't just purchase or obtain the fruits of the Spirit. They are transformational byproducts that overflow from your closeness and oneness with the Lord.

So, if you're in the dating season, please pair Hard No's and Life Enhancers together. If you're going to ask your date (potential future spouse) to have certain qualities, you better be working on yourself too!

If you're not in the dating season, you're not off the hook. You can still do this! We always have room for improvement. Do you want to be a healthier friend? Healthier spouse? Healthier sibling?

What in your life do you want to enhance?

3, 3, 1

Shoutout to my life coach, Michele! We have had breakthrough conversations over the past few years, and we've also had conversations where she listened to me cry for the hour session. Best money I ever spent, even the sessions where all I did was cry. She is the one who implemented 3, 3, 1 into my life when I was in a rough season of motherhood. I was unapologetically verbally and mentally destroying my mommin' confidence. Michele said you are not allowed to talk to yourself or about yourself like that anymore, and 3, 3, 1 was part of my homework for one week. My husband and I continue to do this every night before we go to bed.

3 "I Am Grateful For" Statements

We start with gratitude. Every day, you have to write down 3 things you were grateful for that day. Big things. Little things. People. Places. Things. It doesn't matter. Write down 3 things you were grateful for.

3 "I Am Proud Of" Statements

Next, we move to pride. The good kind of pride. What were you proud of today? ... and yes, it has to be about you. Why are you proud of yourself today? Write down THREE things. This is my hardest one every time.

1 "I Am Great Today Because" Statements

Lastly, we end with greatness. For me specifically, I have to finish this statement, "I'm a great mom today because..." You might say, "I'm a great employee today because..." Or, "I'm a great daughter today because..." Whatever area you're focusing on, you write it out and finish the statement.

In total, you will have seven sentences daily. I look forward to 3, 3, 1 every night because, first off, I get to hear about Grant's day, and secondly, it reminds me that even in the chaos of each day, there is so much to be grateful for, so much to reflect back on, and so much greatness inside each one of us. All thanks to the Lord.

Fill My Cup

By far, Fill My Cup is my favorite exercise. Have you ever heard of the 5 Love Languages by Gary Chapman? If not, take his quiz right now and come back to this spot in the book.

My top two love languages are words of affirmation and gifts. I love giving words and receiving words. I also love giving gifts and secretly (not secretly), I love receiving gifts. I tell my friends and family that I always accepting words and gifts. The more, the merrier. That is why I Sense a Mantra, Mirror Mirror, and 3, 3, 1 are so powerful for me–the words, the affirmation, and the acknowledgement are all gifts to my soul.

Fill My Cup is specifically what fills you up. What makes you feel the most fulfilled. If you're having a rotten day, what do you want to do to ease the irritation? If you're having a fantastic day, what do you want to do to celebrate?

For this exercise you'll need to make three lists. These are exhaustive lists. When you think you've listed them all, write a couple more! I'll add a few of my examples as well.

List One- All the freebies. What do you like to do by yourself or with others that is free and fills your love cup? This could also be items, activities, or products you already have in your home.

Courtney's Examples: Bubble bath, long decompressing shower, home workout, reading, hot tea at night, journaling, baking, and taking walks as a family.

List Two- The things that cost. What do you like to do by yourself or with others that isn't free and fills your love cup?

Courtney's Examples: Buying coffee, buying anything, new candles, mani/pedis, giving gifts, and date nights with Grant.

List Three- New things. What would you like to do, try, or experience by yourself or with others that you have not before? On this list, it does not matter if it is free or not; write them all down.

Courtney's Examples: Make my own candle, host a clothing exchange (in the works), try new restaurants, make new recipes, and go on a Mediterranean cruise.

Now that you have your lists, pull out your calendar. My goal for you is to start doing one thing for yourself each week. Mix it up between the free and not-free activities. Where can you budget in List Three items? And eventually work yourself up to adding 2-3 items for yourself each week, and then 4-5 items, and by the end you'll be doing something for yourself each day of the week.

Yes, it does take some planning and preparation, but investing in yourself is the greatest investment you'll make. You get to try new things. Figure out what you like and don't like.

Fall in love with learning about and investing in yourself. You'll be glad you did.

Declarations

I want this exercise to be the most influential and most powerful for you! According to upcounsel.com, "A declaration is a written statement submitted to a court in which the writer swears 'under penalty of perjury' that the contents are true." The declaration is valid through and through. There is no wavering. There is no questioning its validity. It is the truth, and it stands firm.

> **"**
>
> *Investing in yourself is the greatest investment you'll make.*
>
> **"**

Declarations did not originate in a courtroom; however, they originated from the Bible. Biblical declarations declare Biblical truths that will be the catalyst to your new life. The purpose of a declaration is to officially and formally announce something. It's announcing the end of something and the beginning of something new. A declaration sets something into motion. It's alive and active. It holds power and speaks life into existence.

What chapter do you need to close in your life? What needs to end?

What do you want to set into motion? What do you want to be alive and active in your home?

What needs to start afresh? What is your new beginning?

How to Write a Declaration

Step One: What's on your heart? What is paining you? What are you speaking into existence? What do you believe? You have to determine what is resonating with you in this season. Think of this as a brainstorming session. Not everything has to be complete sentences. Jot notes down—whatever comes to mind.

You can write declarations about anything! Your dating life, marriage, faith, healing, current children, future children, work, finances, etc. You can have multiple declarations going on in your life at the same time.

There are so many ways to write declarations, and I will share with you what worked for me, but feel free to tweak it however you need to. Under each step, I will include my own personal example in regards to writing this book.

Courtney's Example: Book writing. Releasing the book into the world. Publishing. Inspire people to find their voice again. Help people regain their identity, self-confidence, and love.

Point people towards God and healthy relationships.

Step Two: After you know what you want your declaration to be about, write it down. It can be in story form, paragraph, bullet points, or whatever you want. I chose paragraph form.

Courtney's Example: I declare that I am an author. These words are from the Lord, and this story needs to be shared. Readers will break off generational curses, strongholds, and unhealthy relational patterns while reading this book. This published book will inspire people to find their voice again and embrace healthy relationships. This published book will propel men and women towards a newfound confidence graced with God's love. The publishing of this book will release supernatural healing and salvations across the United States. The enemy cannot stop the success of this book, nor can he interfere with the progress, healing, and Holy Spirit encounters these readers will experience.

Step Three: Which Scriptures back up your declaration?

Courtney's Example:

Isaiah 54:17: "...No weapon formed against you shall prosper, and every tongue which rises against you in judgment you shall condemn. This is the heritage of the servants of the Lord, and their righteousness is from Me," says the Lord (NKJV).

Matthew 16:19: And I will give you the keys of the kingdom of heaven, and whatever you bind on earth will be bound in heaven, and whatever you loose on earth will be loosed in heaven (NKJV).

Ephesians 6:12: For we do not wrestle against flesh and blood, but against principalities, against powers, against the rulers of the darkness of this age, against spiritual hosts of wickedness in the heavenly places (NKJV).

Galatians 5:22-23: But the fruit of the Spirit is love, joy, peace, longsuffering, kindness, goodness, faithfulness, gentleness and self-control. Against such there is no law (NKJV).

Step Four: Do you want to include any part of the Scriptures in your declarations or do you want to write out the Scriptures separately? This can be done either way. I have note cards with specific Scriptures written on them, and at the bottom, I write what I'm declaring. For this example, however, I am weaving them into the declaration.

Courtney's Example: I declare that I am an author. These words are from the Lord, and this story needs to be shared. Readers will break off generational curses, strongholds, and unhealthy relational patterns while engaged with this book (Matthew 16:19). This published book will inspire people to find their voice again and embrace healthy relationships. This published book will propel men and women towards a newfound confidence graced with God's love. They will grow and develop healthy fruit in Jesus' name (Galatians 5:22-23)! The publishing of this book will release supernatural healing and salvations across the United States, and the forces of darkness will not prevail in agreement with Ephesians 6:12. And according to Isaiah 54:17, the enemy cannot stop the success of this book nor can he interfere with the progress, healing, and Holy Spirit encounters these readers will experience. Amen!

Step Five: Where and how do you want your declaration displayed? It is important that we don't just write our declarations and then forget about them. Like our mantras, we want to rehearse them daily so they become who we are. Remember, a declaration means it is already determined. When you say your declaration, declare it with confidence and gusto!

Courtney's Example: I printed off my declaration from Step Four, and I listed out all the Scriptures below the declaration. I chose a font and size that was easy to read. One copy is taped to my bathroom mirror, one is in my kitchen, and the other is stationed in our office. Every time I see them, I say it out loud declaring it with confidence and gusto!

Pause:

_____

_____

_____

_____

_____

Ponder:

1. Which exercise(s) resonated most with you?

_____

_____

_____

_____

_____

2. How can you invest in yourself moving forward?

_____

_____

_____

_____

_____

Prayer:

Lord, I pray that my sweet friends are constantly reminded how their lives matter. I pray they will use the strategies and exercises we've discussed in this book to combat the enemy. I pray they don't quit. They don't give in. They don't let the enemy win. I pray they feel excitement for the new season of growth, deliverance, and joy that is upon them! May the fruits of the Spirit in Galatians 5 flourish in their lives! Amen!

_____

_____

_____

_____

_____

Conclusion

Don't Wait for the Other Shoe to Drop

I am SO proud of you! Look back at where we started. Wow. You have been through some tough, scary, and lonely stuff. However, chapter by chapter you persevered, and you made it!

Can we agree that joy certainly looks good on you? Have you felt excitement rising? There's a world full of freedom, possibility, and adventure. It's waiting for YOU!

I want to encourage you one last time. People who are "waiting for the other shoe to drop" essentially do not believe they are worthy of whatever is in their life at that moment. It could be a partner. It could be a job. It could be health. Kids. Finances. Whatever it is, they are timidly peering around every corner waiting for the bottom to fall out.

They just "know" something bad is going to happen. They just "know" they are going to ruin it. They just "know" they aren't worthy.

Do not wait for the other shoe to drop. Do not wait for the bottom to fall out. If you live like this, inevitably, self-sabotage will creep in. You'll move backwards and discount yourself. You'll unintentionally and sometimes subconsciously revert to old patterns, old relationships, and the old you.

Don't do it, my friend. Thank the person you were up until this point. Seriously. Thank them. They helped you get to where you are. They protected you. They nurtured you. They sheltered you. They got you through page after page of this book. Each pause, ponder, and prayer section. Thank them for never giving up on you.

And now growth feels strange. Healthy is weird. It's new territory. But embrace the strange. Welcome the weird. Thank your former self for getting you to this point, and let them know it's okay to move forward.

You get to live a beautiful life. Take that next step. Make that move. You are not bound by that season anymore. And that relationship does not define you.

No. More. Settling. Only. Soaring.

There will always be unhealthy people in this world, but we get to choose who influences our lives. We choose who to do life with and what will be true about us. We don't have to wear the labels or carry the burdens of the lies that relationships dared to mark us with. We wave the banner of freedom and truth.

"

Thank them for never giving up on you.

"

You can embrace new friendships. You can look forward to that interview. That new job. You can experience a life-giving and fulfilling relationship.

Don't forget to surround yourself with cheerleaders and truth-tellers. My husband is my biggest fan and greatest cheer-leader. And I have some of the most incredible truth-telling besties. Keep your cheerleaders and truth-tellers close. They will champion you through this life, and tell you the truth, es-pecially when you least want to hear it but desperately need it.

This is a fresh season for a refined you. Embrace the newness. Inhale the freedom. Step out of who you used to be and keep moving forward. Go on and live that abundant life!

Show *yourself* that you know how to do it! Show others you *can* do it! Show the world *how* to do it! Someone is waiting to hear your success story. The best is yet to come, my friend.

With Love,

Courtney

Pause:

_____

_____

_____

_____

_____

Ponder:

1. Who are your cheerleaders and truth-tellers?

_____

_____

_____

_____

_____

2. What is your next step?

_____

_____

_____

_____

_____

Prayer:

Lord, we wave the banner of freedom and truth. We rebuke any self-sabotage and shake off the fear that the bottom might fall out. We do not accept the "waiting for the other shoe to drop" ideology. We inhale all the goodness and love you have for us. If my friend does not have cheerleaders and truth-tellers in their life, I pray You bring those people into their path. The friendships would be those of Proverbs 27:9, "A sweet friendship [that] refreshes the soul." I pray for God-appointed conversations and timely next steps for each reader. I pray someone's healing is unlocked when they hear my friend's journey through this book. Amen!

_____

_____

_____

_____

_____

Salvation Prayer

If you found yourself reading this book wondering how do I get some of this hope? How do I get to experience this Savior's love? This is the spot for you. Your life can be forever changed by this simple prayer. When you are ready, say this prayer out loud:

Dear Jesus,

I confess my sins and ask for your forgiveness. Please come into my heart as my Lord and Savior. Take complete control of my life and help me walk in your footsteps daily by the power of the Holy Spirit. Thank you Lord for saving me and for answering my prayer. Amen!

If you just prayed that prayer, I am so excited for you! Heaven is cheering! Seriously, heaven is throwing the biggest party right now! I am cheering for you too!

I would love to know if you have made this decision for your life and make sure you have the resources you need to begin this faith journey. Please send me an email with this exciting news at connectingwithcourtneymiller@gmail.com.

Welcome to the family!

With love,

Courtney

A Note For Friends & Families

If you have a friend or family member in an abusive relationship, respectfully, this isn't about you and how you're frustrated about this situation. It's about this person and how they are manipulated and still in this abusive situation. If you were in a similar situation and had the courage and strength to leave, you should be more not less empathetic. You can't be less empathetic with someone, especially if you've gone through this and made it to the other side. It's not about you. How you left might not be the same path as someone else.

Don't be upset about the time you "wasted" and the resources you spent to help them. When you know someone is in an abusive relationship, focusing on their reasoning for leaving or not leaving misaddresses the issue. Addressing the focal issue of violence and the abuser needs to come first.

You planted a seed. The statistics are still there. Even if they left one time and returned, they still heard you! You're doing your part, and they are responsible for the rest.

Don't Be a Bystander

A bystander is someone who watches something occur but does not get involved. Every time the perpetrator is rude, disrespectful, dishonest, aggressive, etc. say something. Sometimes people would tell me that the behavior directed towards me was not normal and was not okay. This was so helpful for me because I was used to it happening constantly! But when someone on the outside saw it and spoke up, it jarred my usual acceptance. The more times this happens, the more times it will shake up what the victim perceives as normal and acceptable behavior.

Other times, people would call out the person displaying the unacceptable behavior. This can be tricky because I have seen it backfire. Sometimes, the abuser is shocked that someone called them out and will stop their behavior (at least in public). But usually, they will resume inappropriate behavior in private. For me personally, I was still thankful when people addressed the abuse in public because they were willing to stand up for me when I didn't realize I needed to stand up for myself (and when I couldn't stand up for myself).

And what I mean by backfire is that sometimes the abuser becomes more aggressive in private. Or they will lash out at the person confronting them, demanding them to mind their own business, or they don't know what they are talking about or to stay out of it. If that happens, it definitely confirms your suspicions that they are a perpetrator of someone's safety.

You might be thinking it's not your responsibility. Or it's not your place. Or someone else will speak up. Or it might be weird or awkward if you don't know them. I just want to encourage you that your voice could momentarily be their voice and help propel them towards a better tomorrow. And if you don't know them, please remember, someone does know them. Someone does love them. Someone would want you to say something.

It won't fix everything. It might not even fix anything. But if everyone sees the grotesque behavior and no one says anything, the abusive actions will continue.

Do Not Blame the Victim

I hope that everything you have read up until this moment proves this point. I hope I don't need to explain further. But if so, please do not blame the victim. How about we address the person making them a victim? How about we hold the abuser accountable? How about we give the victim the most generous assumption on why they haven't left, why they can't leave, or why they have returned. And if you need more advice in this area, please reread the book.

Become Educated

Do some research. Abuse is not subject to a certain neighborhood, zip code, or state. It does not matter if you are from the suburbs, inner city, or country. Abuse doesn't calculate what your home-town's population is before determining if you will be a victim. It does not care if you are wealthy or poor, and it does not discriminate based on education or ethnicity.

Learn the statistics. There are hotlines, resources, safe houses, half-way houses, and organizations in place to help victims of abuse. There are wonderful organizations ready and prepared to immediately help those seeking safety from abuse.

For example, the Family Violence Program of Texas lists every city with a shelter and hotline number in addition to the services the program offers. You can also find which shelters and programs are in your area by visiting https://www.domesticshelters.org/. Please research to find out what your area's options are.

https://www.hhs.texas.gov/services/safety/family-violence-program

And when you learn more about the statistics, please remember that men are victims too. We live in a society where men are seen as weak if they have emotions. They are made to believe they cannot be abused. This cannot be further from the truth. Please do not discount a man's story if he's being abused. And please speak up for him! Don't blame him. He deserves the same amount of empathy, understanding, and love as you would give a woman.

Set Boundaries

This one is so hard for me because, I too, have friends and family who are in or who have been in toxic, unhealthy, and abusive relationships. It didn't matter how much I stood up for them or how educated I was; they still determined when enough was enough for them. And to this day, some of them are still in the cycle of abusive relationships. It makes me incredibly sad every time they return to the toxicity, but I can't change them or make them.

Instead of ignoring them or writing them off (because thank goodness no one did that to me), I had to set boundaries so that I wouldn't obsess over something I couldn't control, and so I could still love them and protect our relationship despite their choices. If this is the situation you're in, please consider doing the same.

Donate

Donate your time. Many organizations accept and appreciate volunteers at various events like drives and awareness campaigns. Each October is domestic violence awareness month. So check with your local community to know how you can get involved, and if there isn't anything on the calendar, consider how you could make your community more aware.

Donate your resources. Many times, shelters will accept clothing and toy donations. Consider for a moment those who have to leave dangerous situations in the middle of the night or at a moment's notice. They might be leaving with just the clothes on their back, and many of them have kids. If you have kids, can you imagine your child leaving without their favorite blanket or toy? Check with your local shelters to see what items they might need.

Donate your expertise. Some shelters or programs have classes to help the victims get back on their feet. My mom is a loan originator, and one time, she taught a class to help victims understand their financial situations and to set a course for them to one day be able to purchase their first home. So, what is your knack? Do you like to coupon or cook? Do you understand finances or insurance? Are you in the medical field or an expert in the law?

Speaking of the law, check out what your state's laws are in regards to custody battles and domestic violence cases. Can you imagine if you're trying to protect not only yourself but also your kids, and you have to go to court to face your assailant in the same room? You probably don't have clothes for court or transportation or childcare, not to mention the finances to pay for a well-represented lawyer.

There are some organizations that are teaching victims how to appear and prepare for court. They help with transportation and childcare. I cannot say thank you enough to these organizations and the people who donate.

Whether it's your time, resources, expertise, or finances, none of it goes to waste.

Be a Prayer Warrior

Never give up praying for them. I am forever grateful for the people who constantly prayed for me. Who constantly prayed for people to be removed from my life. Who prayed for a hedge of protection around me. Even in my worst moments, when I didn't even know if I believed in prayer anymore, I am so thankful for those who did. I am so grateful for my name on their prayer list.

A Mama's Heart
(a note from Brendar)

You fall in love with your spouse, and you think, "Wow, this is love!" Then you find out you're pregnant and you prepare for the baby's arrival. When I held Courtney in my arms for the first time that was a love I never had experienced before. I looked at that precious baby and wanted to cocoon her and protect her from any hurt, any sadness, and any disappointment that might come her way. She was so tiny and defenseless. That love I experienced when she was born has never left; I would do anything to protect my "baby" (who at the time I am writing this is a 30-year-old baby).

Fast forward to Courtney's middle school, high school, and college days. I remember the night I felt something was wrong but did not confront her. As a mama, I knew she was struggling with something or several things, but I didn't press her. In hindsight, I would encourage all "parents" that the Holy Spirit is speaking to you and do not push those feelings aside. Instead, come alongside your child and be someone they can speak to. Speak life over them. Encourage them and let them know regardless of their circumstances that you are a "yell-free/judgment-free zone," but let them know you are also going to speak from a place of honesty and loving concern for them.

When Courtney was struggling in her relationship, I had no idea of the torment she was going through, and it broke my heart when I found out. Why didn't I know what she was going through? Why didn't I pry? Why didn't I do something to protect her??! Well, I did what I knew to do and was equipped to do at that time in my life. I believed "the prayer of faith will see you through."

I was taught Jesus answers prayers and you may not see the immediate answers with your eyes, but Jesus is at work. Galatians 6:9 (KJV) states, "And let us not be weary in well doing: for in due season we shall reap, if we faint not." You may get tired of praying the same, old prayer but do not give up, it will be answered!

I prayed for Courtney's safety. I prayed the people in her life that were not meant to stay would leave immediately and that the Lord would protect Courtney's heart in the process. I then prayed the same thing for her future spouse. I thanked the Lord for her future husband and her future family. Thank you, Lord, for my answered prayers!

Now fast forward to today. I am in a new place spiritually and I KNOW that I KNOW the Lord answers prayer; I am fully persuaded that He answers prayer and instead of it being a last resort ("Well, I guess all we can do is pray...") it is my first line of defense.

Moms, dads, grandparents, aunts, uncles, friends, co-workers... hear me out. DO NOT GIVE UP! NEVER SETTLE! I don't care what it looks like in the physical realm, pray for them, check in on them, and let them know you love them. Do not isolate from them because they brushed you off or told you to back off. Determine that they are a precious jewel. Polish your jewel with words of affirmation and giving of the most precious element, your time.

Never. Give. Up.

Courtney, I'm incredibly proud of you for never giving up and putting the Lord at the center of your healing journey.

Love,

Brendar

A Spouse's Love
(a note from Grant)

Being a part of Courtney's "healing journey," as a boyfriend, fiancé, and now husband, I have witnessed God's hand of grace and love all over my wife.

In the beginning, she built walls around her heart as a means of protection and defense. I knew those walls would take time to come down. I had to be gentle and kind. I had to be aware of the way I talked and responded to Courtney ensuring I was speaking from a place of patience and love and not out of anger or frustration. I was committed to help her work through any "triggers" that arose during our dating and courtship.

As time went on, God continued to heal her, and she was receptive to the change. You could see God's love transforming her. People were drawn to her, and God has given her the ability to sit and listen to them share their hearts. I saw God transform her heart and mind, working through forgiveness of her past. Her heart filled with compassion for others in domestic violent relationships, and I saw her desire to lead other towards the healing she had found.

The way she loved and respected me, despite her past, was nothing but the grace of God. The healing change she welcomed from the Lord has allowed our marriage and family to flourish. It is remarkable to look back at how God has mightily used my wife's testimony for His glory, and how we are still witnessing Him use her.

I believe the most important thing I did (and still do) was simply love her right where she was. I spoke life into her, encouraged and championed her from the onset of our dating all the way through this book writing journey. I declared that God had BIG plans for her. I prophetically spoke over this book, that it WILL touch thousands of hearts and will heal those that read it! May the Lord anoint her and bless all that she puts her hand to.

I love you and am so proud of you, Courtney.

Love,

Grant

About theAuthor

Courtney Miller is a certified health and life coach, writer, and working mama. She resides in East Texas with her husband of six years, Grant, and their daughter Brinley. Courtney is passion about serving others and is specifically drawn to ministering to women, moms of littles, and her church's community group. She encourages people's stories to be heard and is inspired to help them heal and grow through life's difficulties. In her spare time, she loves hosting friends and family, baking, and traveling. Her mission in life is to steward well all that the Lord places before her and to be generous on every occasion.

Scripture References and Recommendations

Revelation 21:4, "He will wipe every tear from their eyes. There will be no more death or mourning or crying or pain, for the old order of things has passed away" (NIV).

Psalm 37:4, "Take delight in the Lord, and he will give you the desires of your heart" (NIV).

Isaiah 54:17, "...no weapon forged against you will prevail, and you will refute every tongue that accuses you. This is the heritage of the servants of the Lord, and this is their vindication from me," declares the Lord (NIV).

Exodus 14:14, "The Lord will fight for you; you need only to be still" (NIV).

1 Corinthians 13:13, "Three things will last forever- faith, hope, and love- and the greatest of these is love" (NLT).

Matthew 5:39, "But I tell you, do not resist an evil person. If anyone slaps you on the right cheek, turn to them the other cheek also" (NIV).

Gensis 1:27, "So God created mankind in his own image, in the image of God he created them; male and female he created them" (NIV).

Lamentations 3:21-23 says, "Yet this I call to mind and therefore I have hope: Because of the Lord's great love we are not consumed, for his compassions never fail. They are new every morning; great is your faithfulness" (NIV).

Isaiah 40:31, "But those who hope in the Lord will renew their strength. They will soar on wings like eagles; they will run and not grow weary, they will walk and not be faint" (NIV).

Psalm 119:105, "Your Word is a lamp for my feet, a light on my path" (NIV).

Psalm 107:14, "[You] led them from the darkness and deepest gloom; [You] snapped their chains" (NLT).

Genesis 2:15-17, "The Lord God took the man and put him in the Garden of Eden to work it and take care of it. And the Lord God commanded the man, 'You are free to eat from any tree in the garden; but you must not eat from the tree of the knowledge of good and evil, for when you eat from it you will certainly die'" (NIV).

Genesis 3:10-11, "So he said, 'I heard Your voice in the garden, and I was afraid because I was naked; and I hid myself.' And He said, 'Who told you that you were naked? Have you eaten from the tree of which I commanded you that you should not eat?'" (NKJV).

Romans 8:28, "And we know that for those who love God all things work together for good, for those who are called according to his purpose" (NKJV).

John 14:27, "I am leaving you with a gift—peace of mind and heart. And the peace I give is a gift the world cannot give. So don't be troubled or afraid" (NLT).

Jeremiah 29:11, "For I know the plans I have for you, declares the Lord, plans to prosper you and not to harm you, plans to give you hope and a future" (NIV).

John 10:10, "The thief does not come except to steal, and to kill, and to destroy. I have come that they may have life, and that they may have it more abundantly" (NKJV).

Luke 5:16, "So He Himself often withdrew into the wilderness and prayed" (NKJV).

Isaiah 54:17, "...No weapon formed against you shall prosper, and every tongue which rises against you in judgment you shall condemn. This is the heritage of the servants of the Lord, and their righteousness is from Me," says the Lord (NKJV).

Matthew 16:19, "And I will give you the keys of the kingdom of heaven, and whatever you bind on earth will be bound in heaven, and whatever you loose on earth will be loosed in heaven" (NKJV).

Ephesians 6:12, "For we do not wrestle against flesh and blood, but against principalities, against powers, against the rulers of the darkness of this age, against spiritual hosts of wickedness in the heavenly places" (NKJV).

Galatians 5:22-23, "But the fruit of the Spirit is love, joy, peace, longsuffering, kindness, goodness, faithfulness, gentleness and self-control. Against such there is no law" (NKJV).

Proverbs 27:9, "The heartfelt counsel of a friend is as sweet as perfume and incense" (NLT).

Book Recommendations

The Wizard of Oz and Other Narcissists by Eleanor D. Payson, M.S.W.

Good Boundaries and Goodbyes by Lysa Terkeurst

Boundaries by Dr. Henry Cloud and Dr. John Townsend

The Lord is My Courage by K. J. Ramsey

Change Your Brain, Change Your Life by Dr. Daniel Amen

Braving the Wilderness by Brene Brown

Rising Strong by Brene Brown

5 Love Languages by Gary Chapman

REFERENCES

Morgan, C. (2021, June 29). My "savior complex": How I got over it. The Huffington Post. Retrieved from My "Savior Complex": How I Got Over It | HuffPost

https://study.com/academy/lesson/how-seligmans-learned-helplessness-theory-applies-to-human-depression-and-stress.html

NCADV| National Coalition against Domestic Violence. (n.d). Why do victims stay? Retrieved on March 13, 2019, from https://ncadv.org/why-do-victims-stay?fbclid=IwAR28o1Ctyyu-mCGJFEzJifjNgq65A3Qlz0teguP-g395V_cb1HTGjtekb9nQ

Definition & FAQ | Stalking Awareness & Prevention | SPARC. (2023, April 28). Stalking Awareness. https://www.stalkingawareness.org/definition-faqs/Raypole, C. (2023, June 12). How to recognize and break traumatic bonds. Healthline. https://www.healthline.com/health/mental-health/trauma-bonding#causes%20 www.stopthehurt.org

Nickerson, C. (2023). Learned Helplessness Theory in Psychology (seligman): Examples & Coping. Simply Psychology. https://www.simplypsychology.org/learned-helplessness.html#:~:text=Martin%20Seligman%20and%20Steven%20F,they%20could%20prevent%20the%20shocks.

BreakTheSilenceDV. (2021). Reactive Abuse: What It is and Why Abusers Rely on It. *Break the Silence Against Domestic Violence.* https://breakthesilencedv.org/reactive-abuse-what-it-is-and-why-abusers-rely-on-it/

Made in the USA
Columbia, SC
07 October 2024

43275721R00100